AF615780

"Martha has written a delightful cookery book of inspired family recipes that are easy to recreate in your own home. The stories that accompany each recipe will have you smiling, laughing, and remembering similar circumstances in your own life I'm sure."

Mark William Allison, MBA, MC
Johnson & Wales University

Stir, Laugh, Repeat

Stir, Laugh, Repeat

Finding Joy While
Playing in the Kitchen

Martha A. Cheves

Tate Publishing & *Enterprises*

Stir, Laugh, Repeat
Copyright © 2008 by Martha A. Cheves. All rights reserved.

This title is also available as a Tate Out Loud product. Visit www.tatepublishing.com for more information.

No part of this publication may be reproduced, stored in a retrieval system or transmitted in any way by any means, electronic, mechanical, photocopy, recording or otherwise without the prior permission of the author except as provided by USA copyright law.

The opinions expressed by the author are not necessarily those of Tate Publishing, LLC.

Published by Tate Publishing & Enterprises, LLC
127 E. Trade Center Terrace | Mustang, Oklahoma 73064 USA
1.888.361.9473 | www.tatepublishing.com

Tate Publishing is committed to excellence in the publishing industry. The company reflects the philosophy established by the founders, based on Psalm 68:11,
"The Lord gave the word and great was the company of those who published it."

Book design copyright © 2008 by Tate Publishing, LLC. All rights reserved.
Cover design by Isaiah R. McKee
Interior design by Nathan Harmony

Published in the United States of America

ISBN: 978-1-60462-818-0
1. Cooking: Courses & Dishes/ Methods
08.02.15

Foreword

If you didn't grow up learning to cook, if you never sat on a stool in your mama's kitchen and listened to her stories of meals and dishes she learned when she was young, if you never, ever change a recipe for the delight of experimentation, *then this book is for you!*

Martha Cheves invites you into her kitchen and her life as she offers up superb dishes with a history. You want to be right there watching as she cooks, shares with neighbors, plans a meal for a weekend away, gives practical tips for the kitchen, and nudges you through her stories to try her banana puddin,' potato soup, country style beef, and on and on. This book is packed with recipes for fruit, veggies, meats, breads, and desserts.

You will never read a cookbook in which the author admits to *not* liking a dish, and then sets about concocting delicious new ways to make it so interesting that she ends up liking it. And you will too! I've already tried and enjoyed her recipe for squash patties.

You will never read a cookbook in which the author encourages you to change the recipe! That's what used to happen in Mama's kitchen. That's what really learning to cook is all about.

Carol Brooks, Ph.D.
Belmont Abbey College

Banana Puddin'

4 bananas
1 box vanilla wafers

Layer in a 2 qt. casserole dish alternating cookies and bananas, ending with cookies.

Sauce:
½ C. sugar
2 T. flour
1 12-oz. can evaporated milk
½ C. water
½ t. vanilla
1 egg yolk

In a bowl, mix sugar and flour. In a medium-sized sauce pan, mix milk, water, vanilla, and egg yolk. Whisk in flour mix. Heat medium to medium high, stirring constantly until mix is pudding thick. Pour over cookies and bananas.

When making double batches of banana puddin, I double everything except the milk and sugar. I use one can of evaporated milk and one can of sweetened condensed milk and omit the sugar. This works great but only when doubling the batch.

> I have several stories about my banana puddin.' Here is my favorite. When I was a kid, my mother would always make this for me instead of a cake for my birthday. She would make it in a metal "dish pan" and pour meringue on top. One year on about my eighth or ninth birthday, my brother and I couldn't wait to dig into it. We would take a fork and lift up the meringue and pull out banana slices and

cookies. After doing this for the better part of the day, it started to sink in the spots we had robbed. Of course, she could tell what we had been doing, so to teach us a lesson she gave us both a spoon and sat the "dish pan" on the table and told us to eat until it was all gone. We couldn't finish it, but I think she thought it would make us sick and we wouldn't sneak around again eating something that was supposed to be saved for the meal. It didn't work. We both still love banana puddin.'

TIP: Peeling boiled eggs? While the egg is still hot. place a paper towel on the counter and with the palm of your hand roll the egg around until most of the shell is cracked. It peels in a snap.

Italian Country Fried Steak

4 pieces cube steak, seasoned with salt, pepper, etc. and flour battered
¼ C. oil
1 jar spaghetti sauce
1 C. grated cheddar cheese
1 T. minced garlic

Brown the steak in oil and cook on medium heat until done. Place steaks in a casserole dish. Cover with spaghetti sauce and top with cheese. Bake in a 350°oven until the sauce is hot and the cheese is lightly browned.

> I'm not crazy about meatballs in my spaghetti and get a little tired of ground meat, but I do love cube steak. This gives you the best of both and tastes even better the next day.

TIP: Cutting strawberries or mushrooms? Use an egg slicer.

Cheesy Chicken and Stuffing

2 T. margarine
4 boneless, skinless chicken breasts
1 box chicken stuffing mix
1 can cream of mushroom soup
½ C. milk
1 C. grated cheddar cheese

In a large fry pan, heat margarine. Salt and pepper chicken. Brown chicken in margarine on both sides. Put lid on pan and cook until chicken is done. Remove chicken. Make dressing according to package. Pour drippings from chicken into dressing mix. Pour dressing into casserole dish coated with non-stick spray. Place chicken on top of dressing. In a bowl mix soup and milk and pour over chicken. Top with cheese. Heat in 350° oven until the cheese is melted and slightly brown.

The cheese gives this a different twist on the traditional chicken stuffing casserole. As you will notice as you read this book, I love cheese!

TIP: Making mashed potatoes for a crowd? Boil 2–3 medium, cubed potatoes. Follow the directions from a package of instant potatoes using the water from the boiled potatoes. Add canned cream, butter, and boiled potatoes and mix with an electric mixer for creamy potatoes.

Coconut Loaf Cake

1 C. butter
2 C. sugar
2 C. plus 5 t. self-rising flour
4 eggs, separated
2 t. vanilla
1 C. buttermilk
2 C. coconut

Cream butter and sugar until light and fluffy. Add yolks, one at a time, beating after each addition. Alternate half of the flour and half of the buttermilk, beating after each addition. In a separate bowl, beat egg whites until stiff. Add vanilla and coconut and fold into the batter. Pour into two loaf pans coated with non-stick spray. Bake at 375° for 30–35 minutes or until toothpick comes out clean. Pop out of the pans while still hot and rub with white chocolate bark to coat.

> My sister always tries to give her employees something home-cooked for Christmas. One year she didn't have time so I offered. We went to the pottery store near my home and bought a bunch of the small, individual, decorative loaf pans and I made about twenty of these small cakes. This cake takes a little more time to make but the results are well worth it, especially if you like coconut.

TIP: When icing a 2-layer or more cake, ice the sides and tops of each layer and then stack.

Spicy Chicken Salad Spread

1 lb. wafer-sliced buffalo chicken breast (from deli), chopped
3–4 T. mayonnaise (mix should be barely creamy)
1 T. sweet pickle relish

Mix together. Makes a good spicy spread for crackers. Yields about 1 C.

> I first tried buffalo chicken breast when my sister bought some while we were shopping together one day. We went back to my house and made sandwiches with it, and it was terrible so she left the rest with me to dispose of. There was no way I was going to throw away a whole pound of meat, so I started experimenting with it and came up with this spread. I don't like it as a sandwich but it makes a great spread for crackers.

TIP: When making meatloaf, try using seasoned stuffing mix to add a little extra flavor instead of breadcrumbs.

Stuffed Cube Steak Rolls

1 small green pepper, cut into strips
1 small onion, sliced and separated into rings
1 minced garlic clove
1 T. vegetable oil
¾ C. stuffing mix
2 T. grated cheese
2 large cube steaks (about ¾ lb.)
¼ C. hot water
1 bouillon cube

In a skillet, sauté peppers, onion, and garlic in oil until crisp-tender. Remove and set aside. Combine stuffing and cheese. Spoon onto the center of the steaks. Roll up tucking in ends and secure with a toothpick. In the same skillet, cook steak rolls until browned. In a bowl, combine water and bouillon. Pour over the steak rolls. Cover and simmer about 25–30 minutes or until meat is no longer pink. Occasionally spoon drippings over the rolls. Serves 2.

> Now and then I like to get "fancy" with my cooking but still want to keep it simple. One day I wanted to impress my significant other and this is what I came up with.

TIP: Try storing brown sugar in the freezer. Take it out about half an hour before using to let it soften.

Rice Crispy Cake

5 C. rice crispy cereal
5 ½ C. small marshmallows
¼ C. butter
1 C. white chocolate chips
1 C. mixed salted nuts

Melt butter and marshmallows in microwave or double boiler. Pour cereal, nuts, and chips into *large* bowl and mix. Spray a Bundt pan with non-stick spray. Pour mixture into pan, pressing it firmly into the pan. Cool. Pop out onto cake plate. Will slice like a cake.

> I was watching the food station one night and the host was talking about his mother making Rice Crispy Cakes instead of making the traditional squares. I took a twist on it and added the white chocolate chips and salted nuts. The combination of sweet and salty makes it great. All of my food testers loved it. You can also use the fruit flavored rice cereal to give it color, but it really makes it a lot sweeter.

TIP: To clean a barbecue grill rack, place it on the lawn overnight. The dew will loosen burned-on grease.

Steak and Potatoes

1 to 1 ½ lb. steak, cut into ¼" strips
4 medium potatoes, cut into small chunks
1 small onion, cut into small chunks
1 t. Italian herbs
¼ C. olive oil
2 T. dry onion soup mix

Place all ingredients into large fry pan and slowly cook on medium heat until meat and potatoes are done. Turn heat up to medium high and lightly brown. Salt and pepper to taste. Serves 4–6.

> My significant other, like most men in the South, is a meat and potato guy and doesn't always want to try something different but he really liked this one.

TIP: Peach measurements: 1 lb. of frozen or canned peaches is equal to approximately 3 medium peaches. 3 medium peaches will produce about 3 C. sliced or 2 ¼ C. chopped peaches.

Easy Canned Green Beans

1 can French-cut green beans
1 small piece salt pork (½"x1")

Don't drain the beans. Pour into small sauce pan, add salt pork, and boil until most of the water is gone. Serves 2–4.

> I love green beans and hate serving the ones that come in a can, but I don't always have time to cook fresh or even frozen green beans. This simple trick will make them taste like they are fresh. This also works on Lima beans too. Add mushrooms or pearl onions or both.

TIP: When a recipe calls for a baking dish, it's referring to glass. When it calls for a baking pan, it's referring to metal. When using a glass baking dish in a recipe that calls for metal, lower the oven temperature by 25° to avoid overbaking and overbrowning.

Chuck's Fruit Salad

1 Granny Smith apple
1 fresh pineapple
1 Kiwi
3 peaches
15–20 strawberries
½ C. nuts, unsalted (pecans, walnuts, etc.)
1 can frozen daiquiri mix (strawberry or peach)

In a large bowl, cut up fruit into small pieces. Add nuts. Pour frozen daiquiri mix over fruit and set aside until mix melts. Stir and refrigerate.

> I had a get together one year for some of my friends in the condos where I live. Everyone was to bring a dish. The friend who brought this dish couldn't have made a better choice. It's great. I've experimented with it several times changing up the fruit, and it seems no matter what you add or take away, it's perfect.

TIP: Au gratin means to top with crumbs and/or cheese and brown in the oven under the broiler.

Shrimp and Rice

1 lb. shrimp, shelled and deveined
½ t. Blackened Redfish seasoning (Chef Paul Prudhommes)

Mix together and set aside.

¾ C. uncooked white rice
½ t. olive oil

Cook according to package, adding olive oil.

Sauté:
1 stick butter
3 T. minced garlic

Add shrimp to butter/garlic and ½ C. white wine. Cook until shrimp is pink. Serve over rice. Serves 4–6.

> My significant other, John, is a member of the VFW and they had planned a cooking contest. I worked for weeks experimenting with shrimp to have what I hoped to be the winner. The VFW is made up mostly of men so the contest never came off, but I will always believe this recipe would have won.

TIP: Need chicken broth? After boiling chicken, place a paper towel (white) in a strainer. Place the strainer in a large bowl and pour the broth over the paper towel to strain fat and any unwanted items.

Meatballs

50 meatballs if served over noodles
100 if serving by themselves
(I buy the charbroiled, fully cooked from one of the "buy in bulk clubs.")

1 can cream of mushroom soup
½ C. milk
1 C. hot water
3 beef bouillon cubes, dissolved in the above water
½ t. minced garlic
1 small jar mushrooms, drained
pinch of nutmeg

In a large sauce pan or slow cooker, combine all above except mushrooms and meatballs. Whisk until well blended and hot. Add mushrooms and meatballs and heat until meatballs are hot. Serves 8–10 with noodles.

> I work full-time but still enjoy having my neighborhood gatherings. Sometimes it's planned on a work night so cooking time is slim. I looked in all of my cookbooks trying to find a Swedish meatball sauce and couldn't fine one I really liked, so I started taking the ingredients from several of them and came up with this. It turned out perfect the first time, and I've never changed it. The first time I made it was as an appetizer but have made it since and served it over noodles. I don't think you can beat it and it's so easy.

TIP: Make extra when making mashed potatoes. Freeze the extra in muffin cups. Once they're frozen, pop them out and store in resealable freezer bags. When needed, pull out as many as needed and heat them in the microwave.

Grilled Cheeseburger Meatloaf

1 lb. 90–95% fat-free ground beef
1 small onion, chopped
½- ¾ C. grated cheese
⅛ C. Worcestershire sauce
½ C. crushed Ritz crackers
½ t. seasoned salt
1 egg
1 T. minced garlic

Mix all together. Form into patties and grill. Serves 4.

> I hate meatloaf! I think it has to do with the texture of the meat when everything is mixed together. But most men love it. I wonder why. Well, to compromise and give my man friend something he likes, plus give myself something I like, I added—you got it—cheese.

TIP: If you have children in the house who need to have their pancakes cut up, use a pizza cutter instead of a knife. This works on French toast too.

Creamed Corn

4 ears fresh white corn, cut off the cob
¼ C. butter
½ C. water
½ C. milk
1 T. self-rising flour
salt and pepper to taste

Melt butter in a skillet. Add all ingredients. Simmer 20 minutes. Serves 4–6.

> I was looking for a recipe for creamed corn, which I love. In the past I would open a can of creamed corn and end up having to add a can of whole corn so I would know I was really eating corn. Not only would it make too much for two people, it was also too sweet. Then I remembered something I used to do when my kids were young. We spent about three months in the North Georgia mountains before moving to South Carolina. I would go out to the open fields and get a couple dozen ears of corn, which turned out to actually be field corn. That's the kind they feed the pigs and cows. But I would cut it off the cob and cook it using the recipe above. It would be a little tough but it was good. So after searching for my creamed corn recipe and failing, I decided to make the good old field corn recipe using tender corn. It's better than great. It's wonderful.

TIP: Need an onion substitute? 1 T. of onion powder = 1 medium chopped onion; 1 T. of dried minced onion = ¼ C. minced raw onion.

Chicken, Broccoli, and Rice

1 large or 2 small chicken breasts

Boil in 3 C. of water. Save 2 ½ C. of water/stock.

1 C. uncooked rice
½ pkg. frozen or 1 C. fresh chopped broccoli
½ C. grated cheese

After chicken is cooked and cooled, chop into bite size pieces. In 2 qt. sauce pan, add all ingredients except cheese and simmer until rice is done. Add cheese and heat until melted. Serves 4–6.

> I came up with this one day when I had to take a dish to a cookout. Money was low and chicken was fairly cheap. But this was delicious, and I brought home an empty dish. You can change this up by adding almonds, mushrooms, or celery.

TIP: 2 T. of flour can be substituted for 1 T. of cornstarch.

Meaty Mashed Potatoes

4 medium potatoes, boiled and drained

Mash with half stick of butter and a 5-oz. can of evaporated milk.

In a fry pan, sauté:
½ medium onion, chopped
1 lb. pkg. kielbasas, chopped into small pieces

Spray a 2-qt. casserole dish with non-stick spray. In a bowl, mix potatoes and kielbasa with onion. Pour into casserole dish and top with ½ -¾ C. cheddar cheese. Bake at 350 ° until cheese is lightly brown. Serves 4–6.

> I love kielbasa, and I love mashed potatoes. So why not mix them together? And of course it has to have cheese. I've not tried it, but I'm sure this would be good if you added onion and/or bell peppers.

TIP: Oven Temperatures
Slow Oven–225 to 325 °
Moderate Oven–325 to 375 °
Hot Oven–400 to 450 °
Very Hot Oven–450 to 550 °

Outside-In Cake

1 box cake mix
1–1 ½ C. flaked coconut
1 C. chopped nuts
¼ C. margarine
8 oz. cream cheese, softened
1 16-oz. box powdered sugar

Spray sheet pan with non-stick spray. Sprinkle nuts and coconut on bottom of pan. Mix cake according to directions on box. Pour cake over nuts and coconut. Melt margarine. In medium-sized bowl, mix cream cheese, powdered sugar, and margarine. Spoon evenly into cake mix. Cook at 350° for about 40 minutes. You can't really test this with a toothpick because it's gooey from the icing being inside, but cake should be golden brown when done.

Variations–Use coconut, pecans, and butterscotch chips with a butter pecan cake mix. Use coconut, nuts, and chocolate chips with yellow or chocolate cake mix.

Add cocoa to icing mix. Use a German Chocolate cake mix with pecans and coconut on the bottom. Just use your imagination to create different tastes using different cake mixes and variations of nuts and chips.

> I'm not crazy about most cakes. They are usually dry, crumbly, and really a pain to make look good. I've had cakes fall apart and fall in the middle. One year I baked a birthday cake for my now ex-husband and held it together with about twenty toothpicks. Then I had to ice it. I hate to admit it, but on the second bite he bit into a toothpick. We had only been married for about three months, and I was so embarrassed I cried. But now I don't have to

ice a cake nor hold it together with toothpicks. I just put the icing inside the cake.

TIP: Before measuring honey or syrup, oil the cup with cooking oil and rinse in hot water.

When my three kids were young, we would have "Mystery TV Dinner Night." Each night when I cooked dinner, before it went on the table, I would take a plastic sectioned plate and put a full serving of everything on the plate, wrap it in plastic wrap and then tightly wrap it in foil and put it into the freezer. On Mystery Night, everyone would go to the freezer and take out a dish. You couldn't peek. Each plate would be microwaved and that was your meal for the night. You may have country fried steak, spaghetti, fish, even chili. It was fun watching the kids open their meals. They were never disappointed because I would always make sure it was filled with foods they liked.

Southern Chow-Chow

Quick and easy!

1 large head of cabbage
8 green tomatoes
3 large onions
4–6 cayenne peppers
2 1-lb. boxes light brown sugar
½ gal. cider vinegar (not white)

Chop all vegetables finely in food processor. Put everything in large stock pot and bring to a boil. Let boil 15 minutes and spoon into pint canning jars. As each jar is filled, wipe off top and immediately put on seals and rings. Place each jar as it's filled on a flat surface upside down for about 30 minutes. After 30 minutes, turn upright and let cool. Jars should seal themselves within 20–30 minutes. You will know they have sealed by pressing down on the lids and they don't pop back up. This is very good spooned over peas and even on hotdogs. Makes 12 pints.

This recipe almost turned into a disaster. There was no way I could cut up a large head of cabbage with a knife and make it small enough for Chow-Chow. I called my sister to see if she had a food processor. She did and even brought it over to me. It was a 1 C. size. Well that would take 2 days to cut everything up so I went to Wally World and bought myself a brand new food processor. I went to work chopping everything, cooking it, and putting it into my jars. They looked so pretty sitting there on the counter but I had a mess to clean up. The last thing I did was wash the processor. I'm blonde, and I guess we are a little dumb sometimes. I sliced my finger to the bone and was home alone. I wrapped it in a towel and went out through the condos trying to find someone home to help me stop the bleeding. I finally found a friend as she was coming in for the night and got her help. The Chow-Chow turned out great and I learned that processors, whether plugged in or not, will chop fingers too.

TIP: Potatoes: *Russet*–baking, mashing, French fries
Long Whites–baking, boiling, frying
Round Whites–boiling, mashing
Round Reds–boiling, mashing
Yukon–mashing

Apple Cake

1 yellow cake mix
3 eggs
1 C. water
¼ C. vegetable oil
2 t. allspice
2 large apples, chopped into small chunks
1 C. chopped walnuts

With mixer, combine cake mix, eggs, water, oil, and allspice. Beat for 2 minutes. Add apples and nuts and beat until blended. Pour into sheet cake pan and bake at 350° for 30–35 minutes or until toothpick comes out clean.

Glaze for Apple Cake

¼ C. orange juice
½ lb. box powdered sugar

Mix together until all sugar is dissolved. Immediately spoon over hot cake. Punch holes in cake with toothpick to let glaze seep in.

> I lived in Anderson, South Carolina, for a few years and there was a fruit stand not far from my home. I enjoyed stopping by there during the summer months to pick up fresh fruits and veggies. This place even had whole milk. If you've never heard of whole milk, it's the kind that still has the cream in it. The man who owned the stand used to complain that he never had business during the colder months. In the winter he would put tarp sidings around the stand to keep out the cold. He would run it all the way up to his house and sometimes even burn a wood stove to heat the place. It

was quite cozy. Then one day he got smart. He had his wife start baking apple cakes, and she was to leave the door open. The smell would float through the whole stand. His apple sales more than doubled the first week. I don't know if that stand is still there. They were getting up in age and this was in the 1980s, but every time I bake apple cake I think about that fruit stand and its smell.

TIP: When slicing meat into thin strips, partially freeze it. It will slice more easily.

Mock Chicken Marsala

¼ C. flour
½ t. oregano
¼ C. butter or margarine
4 chicken breasts with bone. Cut a pocket in the breast but don't cut completely through.
1 C. sliced mushrooms
½ C. white wine
4 slices cheddar cheese
salt and pepper to taste

Season chicken with salt, pepper, and oregano and dredge in flour. Heat butter in skillet with a lid. Brown both sides of chicken then put lid on skillet. Cook until completely done. When done, stuff mushrooms and cheese in the pocket. Add wine and very slowly simmer with lid on until cheese melts. This is good served over rice or noodles.

The first time I ate chicken marsala I was at a little restaurant in the North Carolina mountains. It sure was good. So when I came home I started looking for a recipe. As usual I ended up taking ingredients from several until I had the taste I wanted. My biggest problem came when I went to the wine department in the grocery store to find Marsala wine. I looked and looked and didn't see it. I'm not a big wine person so I really didn't know what section to look in. The deli was near so I walked over to see if someone could tell me where I could find it. The woman behind the counter didn't know either but the man she had been waiting on said he could help. He was a chef at one of the country clubs here in Charlotte and made it all the time. He walked back to the wines with me and pointed it out. I was shocked by the price. It was about $40 a bottle. I love this dish but not that much. He then told me a secret. He showed me a white wine that was only about $10 a bottle and said it would work just as well. You know what? It did and still does. So if you try this recipe, just find a good white wine and don't buy that high-priced stuff.

Beth's Chicken Casserole for a Crowd

1 bag large egg noodles, cooked according to package directions
3–4 chicken breasts, cooked, cooled, and cut into bite-sized pieces
1 can cream of mushroom soup
1 can cream of chicken soup
1 lb. Velveeta cheese
potato chips, corn chips, or crackers, crushed

Pour noodles into two casserole dishes sprayed with non-stick spray. Mix both soups and cheese together until blended. Add chicken to soup mix. Pour over noodles. Top with crushed chips. Bake at 350° for 20 minutes. Sauce should be bubbling. Serves 10–12.

> The first time I met Beth was at a Fourth of July cookout. I was in the process of buying my condo and found that she lived two doors down from where I was buying. When most people first meet they usually end up asking where each other works. I asked Beth and she told me she worked at a jewelry store. She asked where I worked and when I told her I was really shocked. It turned out that her son was married to my boss's daughter. I thought, *Oh no! I'm really going to have to walk a straight line now.* But, we are close friends and I would do anything for her. She is also one of my food testers. Actually, she was my first tester. The first time I tried Beth's chicken casserole was at a condo gathering. I tried to think of a way to change the recipe to make it better, but I don't think that's possible. The only thing I even remotely came up with was to maybe add some Portabella mushrooms.

TIP: Parchment paper is resistant to grease and moisture. Just line your baking dish with the paper, place your cookies on it, and bake. When you're finished, throw the paper away. No mess!

Strawberry Nut Crunch

40–45 crushed vanilla wafers
6 T. lemon juice
1 can sweetened, condensed milk
1 C. chopped nuts
2 pkg. frozen strawberries, thawed
1 8-oz. carton whipped topping

Line casserole dish with ½ crushed wafers. Mix milk with lemon juice and fold in whipped topping. Add strawberries and nuts. Pour mixture on top of wafers. Top with remaining wafers. Refrigerate several hours. Serves 6–8.

> The first time I made this dish, the family and I were going to a friend's house to cook dinner. I was to bring the dessert. I had tried several variations of this and liked this one best. I couldn't wait to get there and eat so I could dig into it. I love most anything that has strawberries and condensed milk in it. We all got into the car and as we were pulling out of the driveway we hit a bump. The whole thing fell out of my lap, landing top first on the floorboard of the car. I was so mad at myself and when I looked at my beautiful dish lying on the floor the only thing I could think about was getting a spoon and scraping up what was on top. I didn't of course, but I was tempted. Now I put everything in a dish with a lid.

TIP: Look for interesting foods and spices at department stores that have small food sections. You will find flavored coffees, jams, teas, and even noodles at reasonable prices.

Red Beans and Rice with Smoked Sausage

1 medium onion, chopped
½ green pepper, chopped
2 T. olive oil
1 t. thyme leaves
2 bay leaves
½ t. red pepper flakes
1 T. cumin
1 16-oz. can red beans
1 can Ro-tel
1 pkg. smoked sausage, cut into ½" pieces
4 C. cooked rice

Sauté onion and green peppers in olive oil. Add thyme, bay leaves, red pepper flakes, and cumin. Add beans, ro-tel, and sausage. Simmer 30 minutes. Remove bay leaves and serve over rice. Serves 6.

> When I was a kid I loved fresh, ripe tomatoes. My mother always had several plants growing and would warn me to stay out of her tomatoes. Well, if you read my banana puddin' story, you will recall that I don't always listen when it comes to eating foods I like. I would see a ripe tomato on the vine, pick it, not even bother to wash it, and eat it. But like the sinking top on the banana pudding I always had something that would tell on me. All around my mouth and down my chin I would have a telltale rash from the acid. She would see it, send me to the "switch bush," and tell me to get a good one and bring it to her. I would but what she didn't know was that before I brought it to her I would bend it enough not to break it, but so that it would break after a couple of swatches around my legs. And yes, I would do the same thing the next time I saw a red, juicy tomato on the vine. I finally quit eating tomatoes. I got older, noticed boys, and the rash wasn't very attractive. Now I only eat

cooked tomatoes. So if you notice a recipe, even the one above that would be great with fresh diced tomatoes, add them.

TIP: Always keep beef and chicken bouillon handy in either powder or cube form. Whenever a recipe calls for chicken or beef stock, you can get by with 1 C. of water and 1 cube of bouillon or 1 t. of powder.

Breakfast Bars

5 C. cereal (Special K, Basic 4, etc. or mix a couple together)
1 15.5-oz. pkg. mini-marshmallows
¼ C. margarine
½ C. peanut butter

Pour cereal into large bowl. Melt marshmallows and margarine in microwave or double boiler. Mix in peanut butter. Pour over cereal. Press into a baking dish sprayed with non-stick spray, pressing down hard to make cereal stick together. Cool and cut into squares.

> A friend of mine wanted me to come up with a recipe for making breakfast bars that had a good taste but weren't as sweet as the ones you buy in the stores. I bet I wasted a half dozen boxes of cereal trying to come up with just the right one. The one above turned out to be perfect. Not too sweet, easy to make, and actually a lot cheaper than the store-bought ones. And you can add nuts, coconut, chips, or whatever you might like.

TIP: An easy way to chop onions and have them ready when needed is to quarter them, put them in a food processor, cover them with cold water, and process. Drain the water off and freeze. These work great in soups, sauces, casseroles, and sautéed.

Basted, Grilled Chicken

4 chicken breast halves

Sprinkle chicken with ¼ t. oregano, ¼ t. granulated garlic, salt, and pepper to taste. Put into covered bowl and refrigerate overnight. The next morning mix together:

¼ t. salt
¼ t. pepper
½ t. oregano
pinch of red pepper flakes (more if you want the heat)
½ t. parsley
3 T. flour
2 T. balsamic vinegar
2 T. lemon juice
2 T. olive oil or margarine
3 T. water
Pour over chicken and refrigerate at least 3–4 hours before cooking.

Grill chicken until done, turning often and basting with the remainder of the sauce. This will make a thin crust so turn the chicken carefully so crust will stay on.

> My sister and I went to what I call an expensive Italian restaurant on Saturday for lunch. To me, expensive is when the ticket comes out and it's in the range of $40.00 for two. Thank goodness she was buying. I ordered a dish, I don't even know what they called it, but it was chicken and really good. After we had finished our meal, the waiter came by to ask if we needed anything else and I said yes. I wanted the recipe for the dish I had just eaten. He went back to the kitchen and came back with a napkin with ingredients written on

it. No measurements because they make large batches so I was on my own with this one. I got it with my first try. The light crust that ends up on this dish is wonderful. So, the moral of this story is ask for the recipe. They can only say one of two things, yes or no.

TIP: If you carry your lunch and get tired of sandwiches and frozen meals, try this. I buy salmon pinwheels and stuffed chicken. Anytime I'm using the oven, I open a pack and throw them in with whatever I'm cooking. When they're done, I individually wrap them and put them back into the freezer. At lunch time I pop one in the microwave and have a really good dish.

Mustard Pork Chops

prepared mustard (good with brown spicy)
6 boneless pork chops
⅓ C. seasoned breadcrumbs

This gets messy but spread mustard all over the pork chops (both sides and edges). Pat bread crumbs on one side only of the chops. Place on a baking dish sprayed with non-stick spray with the non-breaded side down. Bake uncovered in 375° oven for 20–25 minutes, depending on thickness of the chops.

> When I made this dish for my man friend, he thought I was crazy. There again, a meat and potato man. He thought the mustard would really mess up a good piece of meat. He even threatened to make himself a sandwich. I finally talked him into at least trying one. He ended up eating three.

TIP: For basting, use inexpensive, small paint brushes. They wash well in the dishwasher or you can just throw them away.

Garlic Potatoes with Ham and Broccoli

6 small red potatoes, washed and cut into wedges
2 T. vegetable oil
1 16-oz. pkg. frozen broccoli, cut up and partially thawed
1 C. cooked ham, cubed
1 envelope garlic and herb seasoning mix
¼ C. water

In a large frying pan, cook potatoes in oil over medium heat until they are lightly browned. Stir in broccoli, ham, and seasoning mix. Add water and reduce heat to low. Cook covered about 25 minutes or until potatoes are tender. Serves 4.

> When I told some of my testers about this recipe they thought the potatoes and ham would be good and the potatoes and broccoli would be good, but to put it all together with garlic wouldn't work. So I told them I would leave out the garlic. I didn't tell the whole truth. I put the garlic in. They loved it. Other veggies can be added with the broccoli such as carrots, onions, or celery.

TIP: Cut up leftover meats, stir fry with veggies, and add a little soy sauce. Serve over rice.

Sugar Bar Cookies

1 refrigerator roll sugar cookies or 1 box sugar cookie mix, mixed like package directions
1 8-oz. pkg. cream cheese, softened
1 egg
½ C. sugar
½ C. chopped nuts
½ C. white chocolate chips

In a 13" casserole dish sprayed with non-stick spray, press half of the cookie mix evenly into the dish. Mix cream cheese, egg, and sugar until smooth. Spread over the cookie mix. Sprinkle nuts and chips over the cream cheese mix. Crumble the other half of the cookie mix over nuts and chips. Bake in 350° oven for 25–30 minutes. Cool before cutting into bars.

> I'm a terrible cookie maker but love chewy cookies. I can remember only one time that I made good cookies. They weren't chewy but they had enough icing on them that it didn't matter. These I made with my kids one Christmas, and they were made by rolling the dough into pencil size strings. Then you shaped them into trees, wreaths, and stockings. They really were a lot of fun for both me and the kids to make. But I lost the recipe and have never found it in any cookbook since. So I've experimented with different batters and always seem to fail with my cookies. My problem is when the recipe says to bake 10–12 minutes, I have a blockage in my brain that says that isn't long enough. They always look doughy and not done so I let them cook longer. So, like my cake story I decided to find a cookie that I couldn't overcook and that's when I came up with my sugar bar cookies. They are soft, chewy, and perfect.

TIP: Meat Servings:

1 lb. with small amount of bone–3 servings

1 lb. with large amount of bone and some fat–2 servings

1 lb. boneless–4 servings

Herb-Basted Chicken

1 T. fresh basil, chopped
1 T. fresh thyme, chopped
1 T. chives, chopped
¼ C. Dales Marinade
2 T. flour
6 chicken strips

Mix all herbs and Dale's in a bowl. Baste chicken in mix. Remove chicken and add flour to the bowl. Rebaste chicken and grill. Baste chicken while on grill. Cook until done.

> I love to cook with fresh herbs and enjoy growing my own when I can. But I live in a condo and gardens are really a no-no. For all of you that are in my situation, I've found a way around this. I hide my herbs. I have sage and dill growing on my front stoop right now. I planted them in large pots and "hid" them by putting fake ivy around them so they wouldn't be spotted so easily. I even have a couple of bell pepper plants growing out there that if you walk by, you would think is also ivy. I did plant a rosemary plant near the back of my building. I planted pretty flowers there ever year for everyone to enjoy. I just didn't know rosemary got so big. I get by with it through telling everyone to help themselves to the plant. "Where there is a will, there is a way." Actually, all of the board members know about my herbs and think the ivy trick is cute. They all use it as a joke, watching what I'm going to plant next. They also enjoy the goodies I pass around.

TIP: When cooking cream soups, *never* let them come to a boil. Boiling causes the soup to stick and scorch.

Potato Soup

6 medium potatoes, cut into small cubes
6 C. water
salt and pepper to taste
½ - ¾ C. instant potatoes
1 T. dried onions
1 C. sour cream
1 C. cheese
1 can drained Portobella mushrooms
6–8 pieces cooked bacon, crumbled

Boil potatoes until almost done. To test, stick a fork in one of the potatoes and it should still feel a little firm. Add instant potatoes and dried onions and cook low until potatoes are done. If the liquid is too thin, add more instant potatoes. Add sour cream, cheese, mushrooms, and bacon. Stir over low heat until cheese is melted and sour cream is blended.

> Potato soup is one of my favorite soups. I worked on this recipe for about three months. I know my tasters were getting tired of it by the time I finally found the right combination. But now, everyone that has tried it keeps asking when I'm going to make more.

TIP: I've always bought the traditional white rice until my sister Net turned me on to Indian Basmati rice. It has a nutty taste that adds flavor to any dish. So try a new rice with your dishes.

Key Lime Pie

2 whole eggs plus 1 egg yolk
1 14-oz. can sweetened, condensed milk
½ C. key lime juice or ½ C. fresh squeezed key lime juice
2 T. water
1 graham cracker crust

Whisk eggs and yolk until blended. Add milk and beat until combined. Add lime juice and water, blend well. Pour into crust. Bake at 350° for 20 minutes or until almost set in the center. Cool and refrigerate 4 hours before serving.

> I took a trip one year to Key West. This was a real experience for me. In Key West anything goes. When we got to the hotel around two in the afternoon, the lobby was packed with "queens" in full drag. It turned out the owner had died and they were having a wake for him. Well for the delay they upgraded us to the best room in the place. Key West has a lot to see and is really very interesting. The food choices remind me of being on a cruise ship. But the one thing I had promised myself to try was key lime pie. I'm not a lime person, but I wanted to give it a try anyway. It was everything I had heard. Sweet, yet tart. So when I came home the search for the perfect recipe started. The combination above is the closest to what I ate in Key West.

TIP: If you want to peel a tomato easily, wash it and drop it into very hot water (almost boiling). Leave the tomato in the water for about 30 seconds. Take out, cool in cold water. The skin peels right off.

Sausage Cookies

2 lb. hot sausage, cooked, crumbled, and drained
2 C. finely shredded cheddar cheese
2 C. finely shredded mozzarella cheese
2 C. biscuit mix

Mix all ingredients and shape into 1 ½"–2" balls. Bake at 325° for 20–25 minutes, or until lightly browned. Store in tight, covered container. Serve hot or at room temperature. Add another flavor by pressing a pecan half in the center of each cookie before baking.

> I had a hard time coming up with a name for this recipe. I wanted it to be something a little different because it has my favorite ingredients in it: cheese and more cheese. Then it hit me. Cookies don't have to be sweet. And putting the pecan in the center makes it even look like a cookie. But one thing I did find out was that when baking sausage, it loses some of its heat and that's why I use hot sausage so it will retain at least a little. Or maybe it's just all the cheese that tones down the heat. Either way, they are really good.

TIP: When a recipe says "fold-in," it means to add beaten ingredients, like whipped cream and egg whites, by folding them in using a down, up, and over motion.

No Bake Cookies

1 stick butter
2 C. sugar
½ C. milk
2 ½ T. powder cocoa
1 C. chunky peanut butter
1 tsp vanilla
¾ C. coconut
3 C. uncooked oatmeal

Put butter, sugar, milk, and cocoa in a small pot and bring to a low boil, stirring constantly for about 5 minutes. Take off the heat and add peanut butter, vanilla, coconut, and oats. Stir until the oats are saturated with the sauce. Roll into desired size balls and press flat on a piece of waxed paper. Cool 30 minutes before serving.

> The cookie recipe above is one from my daughter Leslie so I can't take credit for it. I'm not a chocolate lover but I do love white chocolate and when I come up with a way to change the cocoa powder to white chocolate I'll change this one. I'm still working on it.

TIP: Keep nuts in the refrigerator. They last longer.

Monkey Bread

20–25 frozen Parkerhouse rolls, thawed
¼ C. sugar
½ C. chopped pecans
½ C. melted butter
1 C. brown sugar
1 3 ¾-oz. pkg. butterscotch pudding (not instant)
2 t. cinnamon

Spray tube pan with non-stick spray. Mix sugars, pudding mix (dry), and cinnamon together. Sprinkle ¼ C. of sugar mix into tube pan. Sprinkle half the pecans over this. Mix the remaining pecans into the sugar mix. Dip each roll into the melted butter and then roll into the sugar mix. Place them evenly in the tube pan. Pour any remaining butter and sugar mix over the top of the rolls. Place tube pan in a warm area until the rolls double in size but don't let them come over the top of the pan. Cook in preheated 350° oven for 30–40 minutes or until well browned. Serve warm.

> When I first started working on the monkey bread recipe, I wasted enough rolls to feed half the hungry kids in Charlotte. I liked using the butterscotch pudding and really wanted to make it work. But I couldn't seem to get all the rolls to cook. Especially those near the center of the pan. After a dozen tries, it dawned on me. I was packing them too tightly. They weren't getting the heat needed to cook them. So if you try this recipe, place the rolls lightly on top of each other.

TIP: To keep lemons and limes fresh, place them in a jar with a lid in the refrigerator.

Breakfast Cups

2 C. grated potatoes, rinsed, drained, and squeezed dry
1 egg, slightly beaten
¼ t. salt
⅛ t. pepper
1 lb. cooked, crumbled, drained hot sausage
1 C. grated cheddar cheese

Mix potatoes, egg, salt, and pepper together. Spray muffin pan with non-stick spray. Place potatoes around the edges and bottom of each muffin cup, leaving an opening in the center. Cook in a 375° oven for 20–25 minutes, or until golden brown on the bottom. Mix sausage and cheese. Spoon into the potato muffins. Bake another 5–10 minutes, or until the cheese is bubbly and melted. Let sit about 5 minutes before removing from the pan. Serve warm. These keep well and microwave easily.

> This was a big hit with my food testers who came for weekend coffee. I also made enough to take to work and they were enjoyed there too.

TIP: Make your own breadcrumbs. Place dry bread, croutons, or crackers (any kind) in a plastic bag, squeeze the air out, and crush. You can also add your own herbs to season them with.

Imitation Scallop Bake

½ C. chopped onion
¼ C. chopped bell pepper
½ stick butter
1 T. flour
½ 13-oz. can evaporated milk
1 egg yolk
1 lb. imitation crab meat, cut into bite-sized pieces
½ lb. shredded cheese

Sauté onion and bell pepper in butter. Blend in flour and gradually stir in the milk. Blend in the egg yolk and cook 5 minutes (add more milk if needed, should be the consistency of gravy). Place the crab meat in a 2-qt. casserole dish sprayed with non-stick cooking spray. Pour sauce over meat and sprinkle with cheese. Bake at 375° for 10–15 minutes until cheese is melted and starting to brown. Serves 4.

> My girlfriends and I go out once in a while on weekends for dinner. We usually end up at either a salad bar, Mexican restaurant, or a Chinese restaurant. If it's Chinese, it has to be a buffet. And if it's a costly restaurant, it must have all the extras like crab legs and shrimp in all forms. We all love seafood and this is the cheapest way to get it. At one of our favorite pricey buffet restaurants they had something new—"Crab Bake." I always try a little of everything that I can get on my first plate so I only took about a tablespoon full. When I went back with my second plate I got a good bit more. But with the third plate I got a good-sized wedge. By this time I decided to see if I could determine what was in it. And if I didn't get the ingredients exactly by their recipe, I came really close with the above recipe. The only difference is it tastes more like scallops than it does crab. But, I like scallops too so that's what I'm calling it.

TIP: Buy your rice at a health food store or any store that offers organic foods by the pound. The rice is fresher, you can buy as much as you want, and the price is usually cheaper per pound for specialty rice than grocery stores. Plus, you can buy just a little to see if you really like it.

Gravy

My daughter keeps asking me how to make gravy. This is the simplest recipe I could come up with:

2 T. oil
1 T. flour
1 C. liquid

Heat the oil over medium-high heat, add the flour, and stir until it's creamy but not lumpy and the flour is starting to turn brown. Slowly add your liquid and keep stirring. A whisk really works better to keep it smooth. Continue to heat until it reaches the thickness of gravy. As your liquid you can use milk for milk gravy or chicken or beef broth. If you've fried meat, you can drain all but about 2 T. of the grease out of the pan and use this instead of adding oil. This will also pick up the bits of meat left in the pan and the taste of your meat. Salt and pepper to your own taste.

TIP: Use leftover chili to make enchiladas. Fill flour tortillas with browned meat, onion, and refried beans, top with chili and cheese and simply heat.

Oatmeal Date Cookies

2 sticks butter
1 C. brown sugar
½ C. white sugar
2 eggs
1 t. vanilla
1 ½ C. all-purpose flour
1 t. baking soda
1 t. cinnamon
3 C. oats
2 C. chopped dates

Cream butter and sugars together. Add eggs and vanilla and mix well. Add flour, baking soda, and cinnamon, mixing well. Next add the oats and dates. Drop onto an ungreased cookie sheet and bake for 11–12 minutes. Makes about 4 dozen.

> Every year for Christmas I make gift bags/baskets for my food testers. It's fun and it's another way for them to test a new recipe. I go to the stores that advertise everything for one dollar, pick up little baskets or cute bags, and fill them with homemade goodies, sweet of course. Last year I decided to again try my luck at making cookies. I found a basic oatmeal cookie recipe and started adding things to it. Of course I wanted them to come out chewy and they came out hard. I overcooked again. They were the last thing I made for the baskets and I really debated as to putting them in with all the other goodies, but I needed something to fill the space. I put them in and ended up with more people calling for that recipe than anything else I've made.

TIP: Leftover spaghetti sauce can be spread over a piece of French bread, topped with cheese, and toasted to make pizza. You can even put it in small freezer bags (snack size), freeze and make yourself a pizza anytime you want one. Feel free to add other ingredients such as pepperoni, mushrooms, etc.

Hamburger Broccoli Casserole

3 medium potatoes, cut into circles
1 lb. ground beef
10 oz. frozen broccoli
1 small can French fried onions
1 can cream mushroom soup
1 C. cheddar cheese
salt and pepper to taste

Spray casserole dish with non-stick cooking spray. Line potatoes in dish and spray top of potatoes with non-stick and salt to taste. Bake at 400° until done and brown. Brown ground beef and drain. In a large bowl combine beef, soup, half of the cheese, salt, and pepper. Pour over top of potatoes and bake 20 minutes. Top with other half of the cheese and French fried onions. Bake 5 more minutes or until cheese has melted. Serves 4–6.

> I started experimenting with this when my kids were still very young. Being kids, they didn't want anything to do with broccoli and would refuse to eat it. To get them to try this I told them the story *Green Eggs and Ham*. Did they know how the eggs got green? Food coloring. You can also put food coloring in potatoes. Now I didn't say that was what I had done and that the broccoli was really potatoes with green food coloring but kids have creative minds that can run wild. They ate their "green potatoes" and enjoyed it.

TIP: Make quick, easy grilled cheese sandwiches using a waffle iron or a Foreman type grill. Instead of putting butter/margarine on the bread, spray it with non-stick spray.

Potato and Ham Soup

6 medium or 4 large baking potatoes, peeled and cubed
1 thick slice of ham, diced
½ C. butter
1 C. grated cheese
1 C. sour cream
instant potatoes for thickening
seasoned garlic salt, regular salt and pepper to taste

Place potatoes in large pot and add enough water to cover about an inch over the potatoes. Cook on medium-high until tender. Lower heat to medium. Add ham, sour cream, and enough instant potatoes to thicken the water to desired thickness. Fold in cheese and season with garlic salt, salt, and pepper.

The company I work for has a service department that is housed in another building. I often bring new recipes into the office for my testers to try and usually call over to the service department to let them know there is something new. But sometimes they are late getting here and it's gone. I received a few complaints about this one day so I promised them I would make something just for them. I didn't ask what they wanted; I just decided to make my potato and ham soup. I cooked up a big pot and took it to them the next morning. I even supplied the crackers to go with it, thinking they would have it for lunch. After lunch I had not heard a word from them telling me if they liked it or not. I was really getting worried, thinking it must not have been as good as I thought it was. The next day I had calls from two of them telling me they had split it up and taken it home with them. The only one I had not heard from was Glenn. He didn't call me to tell me how much he liked or hated it. He came to see me. He said he really didn't like potato soup but he tried it and liked it so much he really wanted to lick the bowl to get the last drop. Good soup, huh?

TIP: To make smooth gravy, put your flour into a jar with a lid, add whatever liquid you are using, and shake.

Chicken Pot Pie

2 large chicken breasts, boiled in enough water to cover them and chopped in bite-sized pieces (strain broth and set aside 2 C.)
3 T. margarine
¼ C. flour
1 can cream of chicken soup
2 medium potatoes, cubed
1 C. mixed peas and carrots
2 pie shells
salt and pepper to taste

Boil potatoes, peas, and carrots until tender. Drain. In a large sauce pan melt margarine and blend in flour. Cook on low heat till bubbly, stirring constantly. Gradually add broth and cream of chicken soup. Add chicken, potatoes, peas, and carrots. In a deep dish pie pan or shallow ½ qt. casserole dish place one of the pie shells. Bake 400 ° until the shell starts to lightly brown. Spoon in chicken mix and top with the other pie shell. Bake at 400 ° until the top pie shell is browned.

> This story has nothing to do with my chicken pot pie, but it is about cooking and poultry. Turkey to be exact. I was living in Houston, Texas in the 70s. The apartments we lived in were positioned in a square with a nice courtyard in the middle. It was a great place for block gatherings. The men all went fishing one weekend and the women stayed home to cook a dinner for the evening. No, this was not in the 1870s. Someone suggested we cook a Thanksgiving type meal in the middle of the summer. I was in charge of the turkey and dressing. I had helped my mother cook a turkey, but had never done one on my own. I did remember that she would lift the neck part and pull out what I call "spare parts." So that's what I did. I decided not to stuff the turkey with dressing but to make the

dressing as a side dish so I never went inside the bird. Just before the turkey was done I changed my mind and decided to put a little dressing inside. The men came home and dinner was done. There were about a dozen adults plus kids so we pulled tables outside to the courtyard and set up everything. As we were standing around making our plates I heard someone let out a laugh that got everyone's attention. One of the men was digging some of the dressing out of the turkey and pulled out the neck. I didn't even know it was in there. I'm going to let you use your own thoughts to picture what that neck looked like being held up for everyone to see. But I will tell you it looked x-rated. Now I check every possible opening there is on a turkey before cooking him.

TIP: Run a knife under hot water when slicing chilled cookie dough to avoid crumbling.

Brown Sugar Banana Nut Bread

2 C. self-rising flour
1 C. brown sugar
½ C. white sugar
1 t. soda
4 medium ripe bananas, mashed
2 whole eggs
1 stick margarine/butter, softened
1 C. chopped nuts
1 t. vanilla

Add soda to bananas and mix well. Set aside. Cream sugars and butter. Add half the flour and 1 egg. Mix well. Add rest of flour and the other egg, mixing well. Fold in bananas, nuts, and vanilla. Pour into 2 loaf pans sprayed with non-stick cooking spray. Bake 325° for about 35–45 minutes or until toothpick comes out clean.

> I do have another short banana pudding story. I went to visit my son while he was in boot camp at Ft. Jackson, SC. He was graduating and to celebrate I asked if there was something he would like me to bring him. First thing out of his mouth was Banana Puddin. I made a very large container, assuming it would be enough for him to share with some of his buddies. The first thing that kid did when he got his hands on his favorite dessert was start eating. I don't even know where the spoon came from unless he brought it with him. He ate until he was full and took the rest back to his barracks. I talked to him later to see how his buddies enjoyed the pudding. He quickly informed me that they didn't because he wouldn't share it. He ate the whole thing.

TIP: When making anything that requires several bananas, check the grocery store for marked down bananas. The fresh ones are usually not ripe enough and the marked down ones are usually perfect for puddings and breads.

Ham and Cheese Quiche

2 large eggs
½ C. mayonnaise
½ C. milk
1 T. cornstarch
2 C. shredded cheese
⅓ C. thinly chopped onion
1 C. diced ham
½ bell pepper, chopped thin
⅛ t. pepper
1 10" pie shell

Sauté onions and peppers until onions are transparent. With mixer, beat eggs until well blended. Add mayonnaise, milk, cornstarch, and pepper and continue to beat for about a minute. Stir in cheese, onions, pepper, and ham. Pour into pie shell. Place quiche on a cookie sheet or baking tray and bake at 400° for 35–40 minutes, or until a knife inserted in the center comes out clean. Allow the quiche to set for about 10 minutes before cutting. Serves 6.

Ham is something I enjoy, but what do you do with the leftovers? At Christmas I usually receive at least one as a gift. A lot of times I send it to my daughters, and if they don't need it, they will send it to the fire station where my son-in-law works. When I do keep one I will usually have one meal from it, take a few slices off for sandwiches, cut the rest off the bone and divide it up in freezer bags, and store the bone in the freezer to season a pot of beans or peas. But that's still a lot of ham and that's what has prompted me to come up with recipes to use up those pieces I keep in the freezer. I've found that after it's thawed out you can use it in casseroles, grilled sandwiches, and even omelets.

TIP: When a recipe calls for ingredients to be creamed, it means to blend them until they become creamy. I usually do this with an electric mixer.

Sticky Biscuits

½ C. packed brown sugar
½ C. butter
¼ C. light corn syrup
1 8-count roll large, flaky biscuits
1 t. ground cinnamon

Preheat oven to 375°. In a small boiler, mix sugar, butter, corn syrup, and cinnamon. Heat until melted. Spray muffin pan with non-stick cooking spray and spoon 1 t. of sugar mix into each. Press one flaky biscuit into each muffin slot. This will create an indention in the center of each biscuit. Spoon 1 t. of sugar mix over each biscuit. Bake 13–15 minutes or until lightly brown and toothpick inserted in the side of biscuit comes out clean. Place on serving dish and pour remaining sugar mix over biscuits. Serves 4–6.

> Everyone has a recipe for sticky buns, so I changed it up some to make sticky biscuits. I made some of these and took them to my testers at work. I usually make an extra batch of things like this so everyone can have one, but this time there were only six left when I got ready to leave for work. I think I ate two or three too many and didn't have enough. The girls from the service department came over to get some and one of my semi-retired bosses went to their department before coming into the main office. They told him about them. He grabbed a cup of coffee and came straight over to get one. They were gone. First thing he did was come to my office to complain. So now when I take anything to the office I make sure I wrap or package a serving up and put it in his out basket first. Got to keep the boss happy.

TIP: To keep from spilling ingredients on the pages of your cookbook while using, cover it with plastic wrap.

Fried Pineapple and Coconut

2 T. butter (not margarine)
1 20-oz. can chunky pineapple, drained
½ C. coconut
¼ C. shredded cheddar cheese (optional)

In medium fry pan, melt butter over medium heat. Add pineapple and coconut. Fry the pineapple and coconut until lightly browned. Serve hot with sprinkles of cheddar cheese.

> I grew up on pineapple sandwiches. If you have never had one, try it. All you do is take pineapple rings, drain a few of them on a paper towel, take two slices of bread and really load both slices with mayo, arrange the pineapple slices on the bread and make a sandwich. You never get all the juice out and when it hits the mayo it can really get sloppy, but that's what makes it so good. I try not to eat these too often because of the calories. I'm sure there has to be close to a thousand with all the mayo. But I always have pineapple leftover and it sits in the refrigerator forever until I throw it away. I finally came up with something to do with that leftover pineapple. And adding the cheese makes it so good.

TIP: Freeze unused whipping cream and thaw when needed.

Pumpkin Cream Cheese Pie

1 pie crust

Cream Cheese Layer:
1 8-oz. pkg. cream cheese, at room temperature
⅓ C. sugar
¾ tsp. vanilla extract
1 egg

Pumpkin Layer:
1 C. mashed pumpkin or ½ can of pumpkin
¾ C. evaporated milk
½ C. light brown sugar
2 eggs
1 ½ t. allspice or pumpkin pie spice
¼ t. salt

Heat oven to 400°. Cream cheese layer: in a medium-sized bowl, beat cream cheese, sugar, vanilla, and egg until smooth. Spread evenly into the bottom of the pie crust. Pumpkin layer: in a large bowl, beat pumpkin, milk, brown sugar, eggs, spice, and salt until smooth. Gently spoon pumpkin mix over cream cheese mix. Bake at 400° for 15 minutes. Remove from oven and cover the edges with foil and reduce the heat to 350°. Bake an additional 45 minutes. Cool completely before slicing.

My family has started another tradition, which is to rotate Thanksgiving dinner between my sister Net, my daughter Leslie, and my daughter Marcia's homes. I didn't get into this rotation because I live in a condo and they all have big houses. Last Thanksgiving we met at Net's house. Everyone is assigned what to bring, and one of my assignments was to make pumpkin pies. I've never really made that many pumpkin pies so I started looking for what I felt would be the best. I found one that had whipped topping in it and even a cheesecake pumpkin pie. That started me thinking. Why not do a combination of both. And as I've said before, I love anything that has the ingredient cheese in it so I made my pie with a cream cheese layer. My sister hates pumpkin pies so I only made one like this since I didn't know how it would come out. After I left, my niece talked her into at least trying it. She did and loved it. Now I have a new dish to make at Thanksgiving along with my banana puddin. If you would like to experiment with this pie, try adding nuts to either one of the layers. Top with whipped topping. Or why not try coconut in one of the layers.

TIP: Instead of sprinkling flour on the bottom of a greased cake pan, sprinkle sugar.

Artichoke Chicken

Artichoke Spread/Dip
1 14-oz. can artichokes, drained
1 pkg. frozen spinach, thawed and drained
½ C. mayonnaise
½ C. Monterey Jack or Italian blend cheese
1 C. sour cream
8 oz. cream cheese, softened
hot pepper flakes to taste
¼ C. breadcrumbs
½ C. parmesan cheese

Mix all together except the breadcrumbs and parmesan cheese and set aside.

2 C. cooked rice
6 pieces boneless chicken, cooked but not cut up

To cook the chicken, simply brown it in a non-stick pan, put a lid on the pan, and turn down to medium. Cook until the chicken is completely done.

Spray a baking dish with non-stick cooking spray. Cover the bottom with the cooked rice. Place chicken on top of rice. Cover completely with artichoke spread. Sprinkle with parmesan cheese and breadcrumbs. Bake at 350° until hot. (This spread makes a lot and can be served on the side for anyone who may want more on their chicken or used later as a dip. Just remember to heat before serving to melt the cheese.)

You won't believe this story, but it's true. My significant other is divorced, but he and his wife are still friends. I met her, and we finally found that we have a lot in common so now and then we go out to dinner and shopping together. She invited me to have dinner with her at a pricey restaurant one weekend, her treat. When I'm put into the position of someone else paying I'm careful about what I order. I almost always choose one of the specials. This was no exception. I ordered what turned out to be grilled chicken with artichoke and spinach on top, served over rice. I wasn't really sure how I would like it, but I would at least make a show of gratitude by saying it was great, take most of it home with me, and then pitch it. Not with this dish. It came with two pieces of chicken and after eating one it was hard for me not to eat the other, but I wanted to take it home and try to figure out what was in it. As usual, I started looking for recipes for artichoke/spinach dip and pulled from several of them until I came up with own version. The only problem with this is it really makes a large amount but it is great on crackers or chips. I've given this recipe to only one person and he has made it for his family several times with the chicken and without. In fact, his kids often request it for dinner. So it's kid approved.

TIP: Use coffee cans covered with adhesive-backed paper in your favorite color or pattern to use as cookie jars and storing dry goods.

Cracker Bars

35 saltine crackers
½ C. (1 stick) butter or margarine
½ C. packed light brown sugar
1 pkg. (4 squares) white chocolate
1 C. pecans or coconut (or mix ½ of each)

Preheat oven to 400°. Place crackers in a single layer on foil-lined 15 x 10 x 1 baking pan. Heat butter and sugar in a sauce pan on medium-high heat until butter is melted and well blended. Bring to a boil and boil 3 minutes without stirring. Spread over the crackers. Bake 7 minutes. Immediately after taking out of oven, sprinkle with chocolate. Let stand 5 minutes. Spread now melted chocolate evenly over crackers and sprinkle with nuts and/or coconut.

> I have never been a real chocolate lover. I like hot chocolate but not things like chocolate candy, unless it's full of nuts or coconut. I don't like chocolate ice cream, and if that is the only flavor there is, I'll decline. But give me white chocolate and I'm in the same haven as chocolate lovers. So, you will notice that whenever chocolate is called for, most of the time I use white. Do feel free to substitute with regular chocolate. It won't hurt my feelings. The cracker bars I'm sure would be just as good with regular chocolate. The salty taste from the crackers and the sweet from the other ingredients are a great blend. I actually got the idea for these by watching the Food Channel and making a few changes on the recipe they were making. You can make changes too by using different kinds of nuts or maybe using butterscotch chips or peanut butter chips.

TIP: A substitute for a cooling rack is an inverted muffin tin. Place pies and cakes on the upside down tins.

Peanut Butter Cookies

½ C. butter or margarine, softened
½ C. sugar
½ C. brown sugar, packed
½ C. peanut butter
1 egg
½ t. vanilla extract
1 ¼ C. self-rising flour
½ C. raw peanuts

Cream butter and sugars. Add peanut butter, egg, and vanilla and beat until smooth. Add the flour to the mixture and mix well. Fold in raw peanuts. Chill the dough for 1 hour. Shape into 1" balls. Place 2 inches apart on ungreased baking sheet. Flatten each ball with a fork dipped in sugar. Bake at 375° for 10–12 minutes or until bottoms are lightly brown and cookies are set. Makes about 4 dozen. (Don't overcook and you will have chewy instead of crunchy cookies.)

> My father still lives in Georgia where I grew up, and when I visit him I always go to the Farmer's Market near his home. This is a huge building that has foods from all over the world. While still living in Georgia, I took a group of kids on an educational tour there. Our guide showed us unusual fruits and veggies from countries that none of us had even heard of. This place has everything. We were walking through the meat area and the guide was telling us about the different kinds of meats: buffalo, ostrich, some I couldn't even pronounce. One of the kids, they were ages ten to thirteen, saw a package of meat and turned to me and said, "Ms. Cheves, what are mountain oysters?" I knew what they were but didn't know how to tell him. I told him to ask the guide. She had heard his question and I'm sure she didn't want to explain either so she quickly rushed us to another section. If you don't know what mountain oysters

are, all I'm going to tell you is that they come from the pig in a very private area. You will have to look to someone else if you want a better answer. But one thing this market did sell was peanut butter cookies with whole peanuts in them, and I always bought a couple of packs. But since my visits aren't that frequent I decided to make them myself. The above recipe is my version.

TIP: To pack brown sugar, place it in a measuring cup, press down, and continue to add until it's full to the measurement.

Meatloaf Muffins

1 lb. extra lean ground beef (90–95% lean)
1 6-oz. pkg. stuffing mix
1 C. water

Preheat oven to 375°. Mix meat, stuffing mix, and water blending well. Press into 12 muffin cups lined with cupcake liners. With a spoon make an indentation in the center of each. Spoon in flavors of your choice. Bake 30 minutes or until meatloaves are cooked thoroughly. Top with cheese and bake until cheese melts (optional).

Suggested Flavors:
Garlic
BBQ Sauce
Onions
Peppers
Worcestershire
A-1
Salsa

> If you have been reading some of my stories, you will remember I don't really care for meatloaf. But again, for some reason, some people do. Even though I don't enjoy this national food I still have to make it now and then so I find ways to fool my taste buds. By making these mini-muffins I can change the flavor to anything I want and still call it meatloaf.

TIP: Make a snack by using vanilla wafers spread with peanut butter and a small slice of chocolate. I use this instead of eating plain candy, and I like to think it's a little healthier.

Stewed Potatoes

4 medium potatoes, cut into bite-sized chunks
2 ½ C. water
¼ C. self-rising cornmeal
¼ C. margarine/butter
salt and pepper to taste

Boil the potatoes in 2 C. of water until tender. Whisk up the other ½ C. of water with cornmeal. Slowly pour the cornmeal into the potatoes. Add butter, salt, and pepper. Simmer until the water is the thickness of gravy.

> I was talking to my daughter-in-law Amy one day, and she said she was making mashed potatoes the night before and my son Shane came into the kitchen and said that was one thing he had never learned to cook. She told him it was time for him to learn. As she was working up the potatoes he told her that I used to make mashed potatoes and put cornmeal in them. I'm glad she didn't listen to him and add the cornmeal. I explained to her that he had it confused with my stewed potatoes. This is a dish that all three of my kids would eat until every bite was gone. The more butter I added, the better they liked it.

TIP: Bury avocados in flour to hasten their ripening.

Tuna Melt Casserole

1 can cream of mushroom soup
1 8.5-oz. can English peas, drained
1 12-oz. can tuna, drained
2 C. hot cooked medium egg noodles
1 C. grated cheese, divided in half
1 2.8-oz. can French Fried Onions

Mix soup, peas, tuna, noodles, and ½ C. of cheese together and pour into casserole dish sprayed with non-stick cooking spray. Bake at 350° for 30 minutes or until hot. Sprinkle with rest of cheese and onion rings. Bake another 5 minutes or until cheese melts. Serves 6.

> I think I told you I love seafood, except for oysters. I can't understand how anyone can eat the whole animal and sometimes even raw. But tuna is one of my favorites. I would take a tuna sandwich over a hamburger any day. And if you add cheese to it I'm even happier. So why not make a tuna melt casserole. It has everything the sandwich has and then some. Of course you can add other ingredients such as nuts, mushrooms, celery, broccoli, onion, and peppers.

TIP: To remove stains on your hands from cutting raw veggies, rub your hands with a slice of wet potato.

Fried Country Style Beef Tips

1 ½ lb. beef tips or round steak, cut into tips
salt and pepper to taste
flour to batter meat
3 T. cooking oil for browning
1 T. flour for gravy
1 C. water
1 T. onion flakes

Heat oil in large skillet with a lid or an electric skillet. Salt and pepper meat. Batter in flour. Fry on medium heat until browned on all sides. Remove from pan and add 1 T. flour to pan drippings. Slowly add water and onion flakes. Return meat and cover. Simmer for 1 ½-2 hrs. Serves 4–6 and is good over rice or noodles.

> One day I wanted country fried steak and found out I was out of cube steak. I had thought about it for most of the day and my taste buds would settle for nothing else, I thought. Well, after working all day I didn't want to go to the grocery store, even though that is my favorite store to shop. So I searched the freezer and found a package of beef tips. This is the same recipe I use to make country fried steak and the substitute works great.

TIP: Use seedless jams to flavor and color icings instead of food coloring.

Ground Beef Casserole

1 8-oz. pkg. egg noodles
1 can cream of mushroom soup
½ soup can of milk
1 C. grated sharp cheese, divided in half
¼ C. sliced ripe olives
1 T. onion flakes
1 T. chopped parsley
2 lb. ground beef
¼ C. slivered almonds
1 small can Chinese noodles
salt and pepper to taste

Cook noodles and drain. Brown meat lightly and drain. In a large bowl, mix beef, onions, salt, pepper, ½ C. cheese, soup, and milk. Stir until blended. In a casserole dish sprayed with non-stick cooking spray, put half the noodles. Spoon half the meat mixture over noodles. Sprinkle olives over meat mix. Add rest of noodles and top with remaining meat mix. Cover with foil. Bake at 350° for about 30 minutes. Remove from oven and top with ½ C. of cheese, almonds, and Chinese noodles. Bake uncovered for 15 minutes longer. Serves 6–8.

As everyone knows, ground beef is one of the most convenient meats you can find. You can do just about anything with it. But I've never found it in any of the Chinese restaurants I go to. So, I wanted to see if I could come up with something that had at least the noodles and almonds in it. This didn't exactly turn out to be Chinese and don't add soy sauce thinking it will give it the taste of Chinese because it won't. I don't think the combination of cheese and soy sauce work very well together. But it ended up being a good dish, even if it isn't Chinese.

TIP: Place a slice of bread in a box of brown sugar to soften it. In a few hours, it will be soft again.

Coconut Ice Box Sheet Cake

2 sticks of butter, at room temperature
2 C. sugar
4 eggs
3 C. self-rising flour
1 14-oz. can coconut milk
1 t. coconut flavoring

With an electric mixer, cream butter and sugar. Add eggs one at a time, beating after each. Add 1 C. flour and a third of the coconut milk. Mix well. Add another cup of flour and a third of milk. Mix well. Add remaining flour, coconut milk, and coconut flavoring and mix about 2 minutes more. Pour into sheet pan sprayed with non-stick cooking spray. Bake at 350° for 35–45 minutes or until toothpick comes out clean.

This coconut sheet cake ends up having the texture of air. It's so light. In fact you might find out it's too light to take out of the pan. This makes a really large amount of batter. I filled sheet cake pan plus a loaf pan with this batter and was really worried that I would overfill them and they would rise over the sides. They didn't but they did come close. I had decided to leave the big cake in the pan, ice it, and pass slices around to my testers that live near me. The loaf cake I had planned to take to my office the next day for my testers there. Well, when I turned it out it cracked and fell into large pieces. Even toothpicks couldn't put it back together. I took a bite and it was delicious. It had a wonderful coconut taste. I went on and iced the big one and tried to decide what to do with the other one. I had icing leftover so I thought about something I do with cake and ice cream. I mix them together, put them into a bowl with a lid and freeze my little ice cream cake. So I did the same with my crumbled cake using the leftover icing. It worked! I could take out as little or as much as I wanted, thaw it, and enjoy my cake another day.

TIP: Instead of using an egg wash when coating meat (egg with water or milk whisked together), brush the meat with mayonnaise and then dip into the crumbs or flour. The mayonnaise will keep the meat moist.

Coconut Ice Box Icing

1 8-oz. pkg. cream cheese, at room temperature
1 12-oz. pkg. whipped topping
¾ C. sugar
½ C. coconut

With electric mixer, mix cream cheese, topping, and sugar until creamy and smooth. Fold in coconut. Spread over cooled cake. Store cake in refrigerator, covered.

This is the best icing for the ice box cake and I'm sure you've noticed it has a form of cheese in it.

Chinese Cube Steak

4 cube steaks
3 T. oil for browning
1 small onion, chopped
½ large green pepper, cut into thin strips
1 C. chopped broccoli
1 ½ C. water
1 beef bouillon cube
1 T. cornstarch
1 T. soy sauce
hot cooked rice
Chinese noodles

Brown meat in hot oil and remove from pan. Sauté onions, peppers, and broccoli; they should still have a crispy texture to them. Dissolve bouillon in water and add to onion mix. Stir in cornstarch and soy sauce. Add meat and heat until hot. Serve meat and veggies over rice. Sprinkle with noodles. Serves 4.

> I may not have found a way to use ground beef in Chinese cooking, but I did find a way to use cube steak. This dish has all you need for dinner in one pan. And of course, you can add other veggies if you like: carrots, peas, etc.

TIP: Use a plastic bag over your hand to stuff a turkey.

Boiled Cabbage

4–5 pieces bacon, fried crisp
½ head large cabbage
salt and pepper to taste

Cut up cabbage. In a medium-sized pan, place cabbage and cover with water. When cabbage is fork tender, drain water and pour about 4 T. of grease left from cooking bacon over cabbage. Crumble bacon and add to cabbage. Toss lightly.

> I usually cook cabbage by frying my bacon, adding the cabbage, and cooking until almost soft. When you cook it this way you loose a lot of the bacon taste that makes it so good, and I want the taste of both the bacon and cabbage. By cooking them separately and then combining them, you get both.

TIP: Poke a small hole in the bottom corner of a sweetened cereal box bag, shake out the small particles in the bottom over the trash can and you won't end up eating all that sugar when you pour the last bowl of cereal.

Freezer Clean-out Beef Vegetable Soup

Clean out your freezer looking for beef that needs to be used. (Or buy 2 ½ lb. lean beef.)

Cut meat into strips. Place in large pot (Dutch oven) and cover with water. Slow boil 1 hour. Remove meat and strain liquid to remove unwanted particles in broth. Pour strained broth back into pot and add 1 can diced tomatoes (size depends on how much you like tomatoes), 1 T. onion powder and 1 T. garlic powder, 2 bouillon cubes, salt and pepper to taste. Add water if needed to keep meat covered. Cook another 3–4 hours or until meat falls apart. Add half of a medium head of cabbage, cut into bite-sized pieces (optional) and any frozen or canned vegetables that you may like in your soup. Add 1–2 diced potatoes and slow boil until veggies are done. You can also buy a package of frozen mixed soup veggies if you like. This soup freezes well and tastes even better the next day.

> Again, when my kids were young I would do creative things to stretch money. One was to keep a plastic 1 gallon jar with a lid in the freezer. You don't have to use a container this large but that's what I used. Every night when we finished dinner I would put the leftovers in the jar. I didn't put everything in but almost. If we had spaghetti, it went into the jar. If we had a roast, it went in. If it was beef anything, it went into the jar. I would also put veggies of all kinds into the jar. When it was full I would thaw it, pour it into a big pot and guess what: soup. It was never the same no matter how many times I made it. I did make one mistake with my veggies. I had some cooked turnips and put them in the jar. Won't do that again. That flavor just didn't seem to fit into what soup is supposed to taste like.

TIP: When a recipe calls for softened butter, cut it into ½" slices. This will allow it to soften quicker.

Chicken Noodle Casserole with Broccoli

non-stick cooking spray
1 small onion, chopped
1 can condensed mushroom soup
10 oz. milk (one soup can)
2 chicken breasts, cooked and chopped
½ C. sour cream
1 12-oz. pkg. egg noodles, cooked
1 16-oz. bag frozen chopped broccoli
1 ½ C. shredded cheddar cheese
½ C. sour cream
1 C. crushed Ritz crackers
salt and pepper to taste
1 t. sage

Preheat oven to 375°. Spray large baking dish with non-stick spray. In a large pan sprayed with non-stick spray, sauté onions about 2 minutes on medium-high heat. Stir in soup, milk, broccoli, and chicken. Heat on medium heat until bubbly, about 10 minutes. Stir in noodles, sour cream, sage, salt, and pepper. Pour into baking dish. Cover with cheese and crushed crackers. Bake until cheese is melted and noodles are hot, about 10–15 minutes. Serves 8.

> When I started combining all of these ingredients it sounded delicious. But when I tasted it before pouring it into the baking dish I noticed it was missing something. That's when I came up with the sage. One of my testers told me that it had a taste she felt like she should know and that it made her think of comfort food but couldn't place what it was. It was the sage. Remember, I grow my own and cover it with fake ivy to hide it. Condo rules: no edible vegetation can be grown on common grounds.

TIP: When cutting soft cheese, place the knife and cutting board in the freezer for about 15 minutes. The cheese won't stick to either one while cutting.

Roll-Ups

This can be done with many combinations, here are a few.

1 pkg. phyllo dough
1 stick butter, melted

Preheat oven to 325°. When working with phyllo dough, use one sheet at a time. Cover the remaining dough with a damp paper towel to keep it from drying out. Also, make sure you have everything prepared before taking the dough out of the refrigerator. Lay a sheet of dough on a paper towel. Lightly brush it with butter. Fold in half, long way. Again, brush lightly with butter. At one end add stuffing. It should come to about ½" from each side and be no more than about 1" thick. Roll stuffing with dough almost to the end. Lightly brush end with butter and seal. Before baking, brush top of dough with butter. Bake about 15–20 minutes.

Stuffings:

1 small can tuna, drained well
1 T. mayonnaise
½ C. finely shredded cheese

Mix well and form into logs to fit dough.

Brown ½ lb. Italian sausage. Drain well, pat out grease.
½ C. finely shredded cheese

Mix well and form into logs to fit dough.

1 small can pineapple circles, drained and cut in half
Cheddar cheese, cut into strips about 2" x ¼" thick
2 pecan halves for each roll

Place a piece of pineapple, a piece of cheese, and 2 pecan halves on dough and carefully roll up.

The combinations are endless, just use your imagination and create your own, using anything from chicken, vegetables, fruit, etc.

> This idea came, again, from watching the Food Channel. The cook was making little roll-ups, stuffing them with cheese and dried tomatoes. While watching I thought that would be good but I would want a little Italian seasoning. The more I thought about how you could change this concept, the more ideas I came up with. It does take a little time to do these because of the dough but they are so good.

TIP: Use left over dill pickle juice to flavor cucumbers. The taste is not as strong as a pickle but the cucumbers pick up enough flavor to make it taste great.

Leftover Roast Beef and Rice

1 5-oz. pkg. saffron yellow rice, cooked
1 ½-2 C. leftover roast beef, cut into bite-sized pieces
½ medium onion, chopped
½ medium green bell pepper, chopped
1 can French onion soup
3 T. soy sauce
3 T. almond slivers
¼ t. pepper
2 T. cooking oil

Heat oil in large fry pan. Add onions and peppers. Sauté about 2–3 minutes. Add beef and soup. Cook on medium heat until soup and meat are hot. Add rice, almonds, and soy sauce. Heat slowly until bubbly. Serves 4–6.

> This is another try at finding a way to change ordinary meat into something that is a little Oriental. But again, it doesn't really remind me of Oriental when eating it. When I worked with this I tried several bottled sauces. Steak sauce, Worcestershire but nothing worked as well as the soy sauce.

TIP: Instead of throwing away day-old bread, cut it into cubes, mix your favorite salad herbs with a little melted butter, place everything in a plastic bag and shake. Bake in a 250° oven until crispy. Great on salads or in soups.

Garlic Pork Chops

1 C. chicken broth
2 T. minced garlic
½ t. cooking oil
4 pork chops, about ½" thick
2 T. chopped parsley
salt and pepper to taste
1 T. flour
2 T. water
1 T. sherry (can use cooking sherry)
2 C. cooked rice

Pour chicken broth and garlic in small sauce pan. Bring to a boil over high heat. Cover and reduce heat. Simmer about 10–15 minutes. Set aside to cool. Heat oil in large non-stick skillet over medium-high heat. Brown meat on both sides. Pour garlic mixture into skillet. Add parsley, salt, and pepper. Bring to a boil, reduce heat to low. Cover and simmer 10–15 minutes, or until pork is done. Remove from pan. In small bowl, combine water, flour, and sherry. Whisk until smooth. Slowly pour into skillet. Bring to a boil. Cook and stir until mixture thickens, like gravy. Put meat in and heat on low until meat is again hot. Serve sauce over meat and rice. Serves 4.

> If you like garlic, you will love this. I only suggest that if you eat it, make sure anyone you are going to be around eats it too. I actually entertained thoughts of taking a piece of this to work with me for my lunch. I decided that might not be a good idea unless I wanted everyone to stay out of my office.

TIP: Leftovers after a Thanksgiving dinner? In a casserole dish sprayed with non-stick, place a layer of stuffing, a layer of turkey, add extra veggies such as broccoli, and pour leftover gravy over the top. Bake until bubbly. You can also add cheese.

Hash Brown Omelettes

4 medium potatoes, shredded (place in water and set aside)
½ lb. sausage, cooked and drained
4 eggs, lightly beaten
1 C. shredded cheese
2 T. cooking oil
salt and pepper to taste

Heat oil in medium non-stick fry pan. Remove half of the potatoes from the water. Drain and squeeze out excess water using paper towels. Place in hot oil. Turn heat to medium. Salt and pepper to taste. Evenly sprinkle sausage and cheese over potatoes. Slowly pour eggs over sausage and cheese. Drain and remove water from remaining potatoes. Salt and pepper to taste. Cover with tight fitting lid and cook until potatoes on bottom are brown. Carefully slide everything onto a flat plate or cookie sheet. Place frying pan over uncooked side of potatoes and invert, putting them on the bottom of the pan. Cook covered until potatoes on bottom are also brown. Serves 6–8.

Making breakfast is really harder than cooking dinner. If you have hash browns, eggs, sausage, and toast you end up having to cook it in the order of hash browns, because they take the longest; sausage, which takes just a little less time than the hash browns; the eggs, which take your full attention; and toast, which cooks about as fast as the eggs but needs to be buttered while it's still hot. Plus you have a frying pan for the hash browns, one for the sausage, and one for the eggs. Unless you've devised a way to keep everything hot and not dried out while you keep reusing the same pan. I've found a solution. You have all of the above by making a hash brown omelet. You will still have to cook the sausage before you start, but you can use the same pan for everything and it will all be served at the same temperature. This works with bacon too.

TIP: Once an onion has been cut in half, rub the leftover side with butter and it will keep fresh longer.

Pecan Muffins

1 pkg. butter pecan cake mix
1 pkg. instant vanilla pudding
4 eggs
¾ C. water
1 T. sour cream mixed in ¾ C. oil
1 t. vanilla

Heat oven to 325°. Combine all ingredients and mix well. Line muffin pan with paper liners. Spoon enough batter into each to cover the bottom (about 1T.).

Mix well:
¼ C. white sugar
½ C. brown sugar
1 C. chopped nuts

Spoon 1 t. of nut mix into each muffin tin. Top with enough batter to cover nuts (about 1 T.). Bake about 30 minutes or until toothpick comes out clean.

Mix:
½ C. powder sugar
1 T. milk

While muffins are still hot, spoon about 1 t. of glaze over each. Top with 1 t. of leftover nut mix and press down with back of a spoon. Glaze will act as glue and hold nut mix in place. Makes 24 muffins.

> I still have trouble making most cakes from scratch so most of the time I find ways to use those old faithful cake mixes. There

are so many things you can do if you use your imagination and a cake mix. The pecan muffins are one that has never failed me. And if you notice, I put my muffins and even a few other dishes in cupcake papers. This is for two reasons. One, the clean-up is easier and second, especially if it's a cake, it doesn't fall apart.

TIP: To butter corn on the cob, place butter in a microwave-safe flat dish and melt butter. Roll the corn around in the butter. Use the same pan to serve in. It's also good when you mix a few herbs in the butter for a different spicy taste.

Imitation Crab Noodles

6 oz. egg noodles, uncooked
1 T. butter
1 small onion, chopped
½ medium bell pepper, chopped
1 T. minced garlic
1 C. sour cream
1 C. mayonnaise
1 C. shredded cheddar cheese
2 T. parsley
salt and pepper to taste
1 lb. imitation crab meat, cut into bite-sized pieces
½ tube Ritz crackers, crushed

Preheat oven to 350°. Spray 2-qt. baking dish with non-stick spray. Cook noodles according to package. Drain and set aside.

Melt butter in skillet over medium-high heat. Add onions, bell peppers, and garlic. Cook and stir 2 minutes or until tender. In a large bowl, combine sour cream, mayonnaise, cheese, parsley, salt, and pepper. Add crab meat, noodles, onion, and peppers. Mix gently to combine. Pour into baking dish. Sprinkle more cheese over mix (optional) and top with crackers. Bake 30 minutes uncovered. Serves 6.

> My dear, loving friend Dusty has gotten to the point that she watches for me every afternoon to see if she's going to have to make dinner. There have been days that I've paid her a visit every evening with something to test. Her husband has even started asking, "Has Martha come by yet?" When I made my crab noodle dish and took a bowl over for her to test, I walked up on her patio and she had a friend visiting. I told her what I had; she immediately grabbed it,

went into the house, got a fork, and came back out onto the patio. I thought she was going to taste it and maybe even let her husband and friend have a taste. If anyone had even tried to reach for the bowl, I'm sure they would have come out with a fork in their hand. According to her and others who have tried it, this is my second best recipe in the whole book. And only coming in second to the banana puddin.

TIP: Use your lettuce spinner to spin excess water off fresh washed green beans before freezing them. Try this with other veggies too.

Biscuits

2 C. self-rising flour
2 T. mayo
1 C. buttermilk

Preheat oven to 350°. Put flour and mayo in a bowl and gradually add milk, stirring as you add. Continue until all milk has been added and everything is well blended. Dough will be sticky but not watery. If it does come out a little watery add about 1 T. of flour to thicken. Pour some flour onto a plate. Remove all rings and watches. Cover the inside of your hands thickly with flour. Spoon a clump of batter about 2" round into your hands and lightly roll into a ball. If it starts sticking to your hands, add a little more flour to them. Place each biscuit on a flat baking dish sprayed with non-stick. Bake about 20–25 minutes.

> The first time I tried to make biscuits I was only around six or seven years old. See, I've always loved to cook. My mother used to make biscuits the old way. She kept a wooden bowl in the cabinet with her flour in it. When she started to make her biscuits she would add more flour, salt, baking powder, and her lard. She would run her hand around and make a hole in the center and start mixing her lard into the flour and pour her milk in. I really wanted to make biscuits too. So she let me. There were only three of us kids at that time. Me and my two brothers, one eight years older than me and the other one and a half years younger. My two brothers got into a fuss that night at the dinner table. My oldest brother picked up one of my biscuits and threw it at my little brother and hit him in the eye. He ended up with a black eye. I didn't make biscuits again until I was grown and decided to try again. I've tried several ways to make them light, fluffy and still have the taste of the buttermilk and this is the one I ended up sticking with to get what I wanted.

TIP: Pepperoni can be really greasy but place it on a paper towel, put it in the microwave for 30 seconds on high, and then blot it off with more paper towels.

Sweet Wing Sauce

¾ C. catsup
¼ C. chili dipping sauce
4 T. melted butter
hot sauce to taste

Mix all together. Use to coat wings or as a dip.

> I've found something else I'm not perfect at making: hot wings. I've tried baking them, frying them, boiling them, and even grilling them. I think I have the same hang up on them that I have on cookies. I overcook them. But after trying to fry some that weren't really good I came up with my sweet wing sauce in hopes of making them taste better. The sauce is good but the wings weren't that great. I did find out that this sauce is good on fried shrimp.

TIP: There never seems to be enough icing in the pre-packaged container. Try this. Mix a 3-oz. container of softened cream cheese with the store bought icing. This gives you more icing, plus it makes it smooth and creamy.

Creamy Potato Salad

4 large potatoes, peeled and cubed
¼ C. butter
¼ C. ranch dressing
¼ C. sweet relish
½ medium onion, chopped
4 boiled eggs, diced
1 small carrot, diced very small
¼ C. mayonnaise

Boil potatoes until fork tender. In a large bowl combine all other ingredients. Drain potatoes and pour hot over other ingredients. Gently mix to blend.

A few years ago I went up to my grandson's christening in New Jersey. I forgot to tell you both my son-in-laws are Yankees. Scott, Leslie's husband, is from Albany, New York, and Tod, Marcia's husband, is from Caldwell, New Jersey. This was Marcia and Tod's son that was being christened. I got there a few days before the event and we planned a menu for the party after the christening. We decided to make it a southern meal. They did buy some Italian dishes just in case no one wanted to eat southern. I had eaten at some of the diners up there and didn't like the potato salad any of them served. Actually, I don't like any restaurant style or deli style potato salad. I only like mine. The big difference between them is I mix mine while the potatoes are still hot. It gives it a creamy texture and the potatoes are softer. When potato salad is made with cold potatoes, the mayonnaise seems to have a problem clinging to them. I also don't put vinegar in mine, which I believe some of them do. So, at the party everyone got to try a real southern potato salad and must have enjoyed it since I made it using 10 lb. of potatoes and it was all gone before the evening was over.

TIP: I keep my coconut in the freezer and sometimes it seems to be dried out when I need it. This is fixed by putting the coconut in a microwave-safe bowl, sprinkling it with a few drops of water, putting a cover over it, and heating until warm.

Calzones

1 pkg. (24) frozen Parker House Rolls, thawed
1 bell pepper, chopped
1 medium onion, chopped
48 pieces pepperoni
24 sticks of mozzarella cheese (½" x ½" x 2 ½")
¼ C. melted butter
1 can pizza sauce

Preheat oven to 350°. Sauté pepper and onion, set aside to cool. On a flat surface lightly sprinkle flour then brush the flour away from working area (you only want a little flour dust on the working area). Working with one roll at a time, roll it into a circle about 3–4 inches wide. Place about 1 t. pepper/onion mix in the center of the roll. Lay 2 pieces of pepperoni on top of onions; lay a stick of cheese on top of pepperoni. Carefully fold the roll over, forming a crescent and using the tongs of a fork to seal the edges. Brush with melted butter. I like to sprinkle just a few pieces of grated cheese and a few pieces of garlic on top. Bake about 15 minutes or until lightly browned. Serve with warm pizza sauce. Makes 24.

> It takes a little time to make these, but they are worth it. The idea came to me when I was making my roll-ups. When I first started making them I had trouble with the cheese. I was using grated cheese and it was melting and leaving air pockets in the dough. I spend a fair amount of time watching the Food Channel and one of the shows is about food chemistry. I thought about this problem and finally came up with the conclusion that shredded cheese has more air in it than a stick of cheese and therefore, when sealed, the air would have no place to go. I don't know if I'm right in my assumption but I do know that when I changed to sticks of cheese I lost the air pockets.

TIP: Need a lot of cookies for the holidays and have no time to cook? Buy different types and shapes of cookies. Melt white chocolate and milk chocolate bars. Dip either the whole cookie or part of the cookie into the chocolate. Add a few sprinkles of colored sugar and you are done.

Carrot Muffins

1 box pre-packaged carrot cake
1 8-oz. pkg. cream cheese, softened
1 can pre-packaged coconut and pecan icing

Preheat oven to 350°. Mix cake according to box directions. Cream together cream cheese and icing mix. In muffin pans lined with paper liners spoon in about 1 T. cake mix. On top of this spoon 1 T. icing mix. Finish filling about ¾ full with cake mix. Bake 20 minutes or until cake is done. Makes 24.

> Most people like carrot cake, me being one of them. But by now you know how I have problems with cakes. So, again, I used the good old store bought cake mix. I tried making this with the same reasoning as my outside-in cake, thinking the icing would stay in the center. Not. But the results were perfect. The icing went to the bottom and you have a gooey, creamy icing on the bottom. And by using the pre-packaged icing I didn't have to go to the expense of buying nuts and coconut.

Cascades

1 pkg. (10) small flour tortillas
1 ½ C. cooked, cooled, and chopped chicken
1 C. shredded cheddar cheese
1 C. mozzarella cheese
½ C. sliced black olives
salsa
sour cream

This is made using either a waffle iron or an indoor type grill with a lid. Place 1 tortilla on the iron/grill, which has been sprayed with non-stick spray. Top with chicken to within about ½" from the edges. Add olives. Sprinkle 1–2 T. salsas over olives. Top with 1 T. of each cheese. Put another tortilla on top and close the lid. Cook until cheese melts. Serve with more salsa and sour cream.

> This is one recipe that you can change in a hundred ways. Any leftover meat can be used. Veggies can be used. You can use fruit. The ideas just go on and on. And if the tortilla is bigger than your iron/grill, use the same method but put the ingredients on just half and fold the other half over.

TIP: To clean pans with food stuck inside, boil a little vinegar and water in the pan before washing. No scrubbing required.

Shrimp Sauce

½ qt. mayonnaise
½ t. garlic powder
½ t. hot sauce
¾ t. paprika
½ t. white pepper
1 ½ T. catsup
1 t. sugar
dash of salt
2 T. olive oil

Whisk all ingredients together until smooth. Store in refrigerator for up to 2 weeks. Great with stir-fry meats and veggies.

I spent a year trying to find the recipe for my shrimp sauce. I went to a Japanese restaurant with some friends one night and they served their sauce with the meal. I dipped my chicken in it, my shrimp, and even my broccoli. It was wonderful. I'm not shy when it comes to asking for a recipe I've eaten at a restaurant. So I asked the waiter. He said it was nothing but mayo, catsup, and paprika. I thought great, really simple. So I went home and made some. *Ugh*! It tasted like sweet mayo. So I kept searching. Every time we ate at that restaurant I would try to determine what was in the sauce. A few weeks ago, Brenda at work told me she had a really good stir-fry recipe and asked if I wanted a copy. Of course I did. The recipe came from a Japanese restaurant that was here in Charlotte but had folded several years ago. On the bottom of the copy she brought me was a shrimp sauce recipe. I went home that night and made some. It wasn't quite what I was looking for so I made a few changes, and now have one that tastes just as good as the one I always get at the restaurant.

TIP: To measure honey or syrup, spray the measuring spoon or cup with non-stick spray. It slides right out.

Coconut Mounds

2 large bags coconut
1 can sweetened, condensed milk
1 stick butter
1 box powdered sugar
almonds
chocolate or white chocolate bark, 1 large pkg. of each

Mix the first 4 ingredients and refrigerate overnight. Shape into 1" balls with an almond in the center.

Melt chocolate in double boiler. Dip mounds into the chocolate and place on wax paper to cool. Makes about 4 dozen.

> This candy recipe makes a bunch! As you should know by now, I make it with white chocolate. A friend, Brenda, gave me the recipe after bringing me some she had made for Easter. Hers was made with milk chocolate but I didn't have any trouble peeling the dark stuff off. I'm sure you will notice that there is a candy bar that is made pretty much like this so that's where I got the idea of putting the almond inside. I made this for the first time this past Easter to go in the Easter baskets for my testers. But I wanted to get creative so I bought some food coloring and added it to the white chocolate to give it bright colors. Mistake! When melting chocolate for candy, remember it doesn't like to have anything liquid put into it. I was able to make it work but not without putting in a lot of extra work and burning my fingers trying to fold the chocolate around the coconut. I've made this since leaving them all white but I'm sure there is a powder type coloring that can be bought if you must have color.

TIP: To keep cakes from sliding around on their plate, spread frosting on the plate. It acts like glue and holds the cake in place.

Potato Boats

2 baking potatoes, boiled until soft

Be creative:
cheese
sautéed onions and bell peppers
thin strips of cooked meat (steak, leftover roast, chicken, bacon)
sour cream
broccoli

Mash potatoes, skins too, with butter, cheese, and salt to taste. Place into two dishes that are both oven and microwave safe. Top with meat, onions, peppers, broccoli, and more cheese. Bake at 350° until cheese melts. Top that with sour cream. I use a dish that is also microwave safe so I can bake these and serve them later by heating in the microwave. This is a good dish to take to work as a lunch.

> This idea came from Dusty, one of my testers, who told me about boiling baking potatoes and scooping out the insides to make mashed potatoes with broccoli and then replacing them in the shells. Well, my shells wouldn't stay together so I decided to mash them too. From this recipe I've realized that anytime I have left over potatoes of any kind, I can be creative and add whatever I like to create my potato boats. After making these with leftovers I wrap them up, put them in the refrigerator, and heat them up the next day.

TIP: Use an egg slicer to slice peeled kiwi.

Tropical Fruit Pie

2 ready- to-use pie crusts (graham, shortbread, vanilla wafer)
1 pt. strawberries (can use peaches) with juice
2 pkg. strawberry gelatin (can use peach)
1 ¼ C. hot water
1 small can crushed pineapple (juice drained and pressed out)
½ C. coconut
1 8-oz. pkg. cream cheese, softened
1 C. sour cream
½ C. sugar
1 C. whipped topping

Dissolve gelatin and hot water in a bowl. Add strawberries with juice, pineapple, and coconut. Pour into crusts. Chill until set. Mix cream cheese, sugar, and sour cream. Fold in whipped topping. Spread over gelatin mixture. Refrigerate.

> This recipe came about when, again, I was watching the food show. One of my favorite cooks was on, and she was giving out a recipe for a fruit dish her sons always liked. It sounded so good I started writing it down. I ended up leaving it on the coffee table and my precious, four-legged guardian angel decided he wanted to read it. I tried taping it back together, but he must have eaten part of it. I did remember most of the ingredients but not the complete recipe. This stayed on my mind for some time. I couldn't even take a nap because it kept running through my mind. So I started putting together the ingredients I did remember and making up those that were missing, as well as the measurements. The original recipe didn't have a crust but I added one and I believe it had bananas, which I didn't add. But I really think my angel had a better idea in mind when he destroyed the original and that was for Mom to come up with something good and different.

TIP: Leftover mashed potatoes can be turned into potato patties by mixing 1 C. mashed potatoes and 1 egg and shaping them into patties. Fry in butter or margarine until brown on both sides. Add some cheese?

Collards

1 bunch collards, washed and cut up
2 slices salt pork
4 C. water
salt to taste

Put everything except salt into a large pot. Bring the water to a boil and then turn the heat to a slow simmer. Cook the collards for about 1–1 ½ hours. When collards are done they will still have a slight chew to them. Taste before salting since the salt pork will provide some of your salt.

> Remember I told you both my sons-in-law are from the North? My Jersey son-in-law, Tod, will eat most anything. I don't know where he had his first taste of collards but he loved them, and my daughter is constantly asking me to cook him some. I'll make a southerner out of him yet. Most people overcook their "greens," at least to me. They will cook them for hours but I've found when you do that all of the flavor goes into the water and the greens are mushy. I like my way best.

TIP: Exposure to direct sunlight softens tomatoes instead of ripening them. Leave them stem-up in any spot that will be out of direct sunlight.

Chicken 'n Dumplins

2 chicken breasts, boiled in enough water to cover the chicken until done

You can check the chicken by sticking a fork into it all the way to the bone and watch for white "juice" to come out, which means to me that it needs to cook longer. Or you can do it the way I do and cook it until it starts coming off the bone. After cooking, remove the chicken from the water and cool. Put a white paper towel in a strainer and place the strainer into a bowl or pan big enough to hold the water that was left from cooking the chicken. Slowly pour the water over the paper towel. This will catch, what I call, the undesirables that cook out of the chicken. The water should come out clear with nothing floating around in it. Put the water (it's really broth now) back on the stove and bring to a slow boil. Tear the chicken from the bone and put back into the broth. Add 1 bouillon cube, ½ t. of sage, and ½ stick of butter or margarine (about ¼ C.). Taste the broth to see if it needs salt and add if it does. This is also a good time to add pepper if you like.

Dumplins: Mix 2 C. of self-rising flour with enough water to make it sticky. Mix well to get out dry lumps. Using a teaspoon, drop clumps of the dough into the water until the top of the broth is covered with dough. After about a minute of cooking these, start pushing them down to the bottom. They won't stay but this will coat them with broth and prevent them from sticking together. Continue dropping the dough into the broth until you have used it all. Slow cook for about 5 minutes. If the broth is still thin, mix 1 T. of flour with 1 T. of water and slowly add to the broth, stirring the whole time you are adding. This can be repeated after 2–3 minutes if needed until it reaches the thickness of cream soup.

This was one of the items I cooked for my southern meal for my grandson's christening in Jersey. No one had ever had or heard of chicken 'n dumplins. I made a really big soup pan full and it, too, was gone by the end of the night. This is also when I met a man named John. He was a friend of my daughter and son-in-law and we started talking about southern food. We talked for about an hour and later my daughter came in and asked me if I knew who he was. I said his name was John. She said he goes by J3. He played with Tommy Lee. My first brush with famous people.

TIP: Another leftover mashed potato tip. If you want to serve them the next day, simply heat in the microwave and add a small amount of evaporated milk to make them creamy again.

Rabbit Food Sandwich

2 whole pieces pita bread, cut in half
1 carrot, sliced into circles
1 spring (green) onion, chopped top and bottom
½ cucumber, cut into circles (need a total of 12 circles)
4 small mushrooms, sliced
½ C. white cheese
alfalfa sprouts
soy sauce

Prepare all veggies and set aside. Place a fourth of the cheese into the pockets of each pita half. Heat in microwave or toaster oven until cheese is sticky but not melted (toaster oven works best). Place 3 slices of cucumber into each pita half (one on each side and one in the middle, this helps keep the bread open). Add other veggies and top with alfalfa sprouts. Sprinkle with soy sauce.

> When I lived in South Carolina there was a health food store near my office. This is a sandwich they served. The first time I saw someone from my office eating one I quickly decided it wasn't something for me, but she cut one in half and insisted I try. It was wonderful. Now I cut up my veggies, put them in a baggie, put my cheese inside the pita and take it to work for my lunch. If you were like me, just give it a try. You haven't wasted anything because all of the veggies can be dumped into your next salad. Get creative with this too. I sometimes put broccoli in mine. You can use any veggie that you enjoy eating raw to make this sandwich.

TIP: When making pancakes, make a few extra. Place a small piece of aluminum foil between each, place them in a freezer bag, and freeze. Now you can have them during the week when time is tight. The foil keeps them from sticking together when they freeze.

Banana Nut Milkshake Pudding

3 C. vanilla wafers crushed (can use graham crackers)
⅔ C. butter/margarine

Mix wafers and butter. Press into the bottom of an 8 x 11 casserole dish.

Filling:
1 8-oz. pkg. white chocolate and Macadamia chips
1 10-oz. pkg. marshmallows
¾ C. milk
2 C. whipped topping
2 t. cornstarch
½ t. vanilla
2 bananas

Pour the milk, chips, cornstarch. and marshmallows into a sauce pan. Heat on low heat until the marshmallows are melted. Set aside and let cool to room temperature. After cooling, fold in vanilla and whipped topping. Slice the bananas into circles and place evenly over the crust. Pour the sauce over the bananas. Refrigerate 2–3 hours.

> I came up with this when trying to change a regular chocolate recipe into one that would work with white chocolate and nuts. The original recipe was used to make a pie. When I tasted the sauce using the white chocolate and nuts it reminded me of a milkshake, and since one of my favorite milkshakes is banana nut I then decided to add the bananas. Well, due to the moisture of the bananas it refused to get solid enough to slice so I decided to try it as a pudding. And believe me, it does taste like a banana nut milkshake.

TIP: I promise the last tip for leftover mashed potatoes. Form the potatoes into balls around a cube of cheese. Roll the balls in Parmesan cheese or crumbs and broil until golden brown.

Baked Spaghetti

1 10-oz. pkg. spaghetti noodles, cooked
1 jar spaghetti sauce
1 lb. ground beef
½ lb. Italian sausage
1 t. minced garlic
½ t. Italian seasoning
1 C. cheddar cheese
1 C. white cheese

Cook beef and sausage. Drain. Add spaghetti sauce, garlic, and seasonings. Simmer for about 30 minutes so flavors blend. Spray an 8x10 casserole dish with non-stick spray, bottom and sides. Put half the noodles into the dish. Spoon half of the meat mixture over the noodles. Sprinkle with ½ C. of each cheese. Repeat the layers, ending with the cheese. Bake in a 350° oven for about 20–25 minutes, or until the cheese starts to brown.

My significant, John, always ordered baked spaghetti when we would go to our local cafeteria for dinner, so I decided that since he loved it so much I would start making it for him. He never orders it now when we go to the cafeteria. I've found that spaghetti sauce in the jar is really good as a base. Who has time to spend cooking the all-day kind? With the jar type you can add herbs, a little garlic, mushrooms, onions, a few black olives or whatever you like and you have a delicious sauce in no time. I almost forgot to tell you about cooking spaghetti when my kids were young. I would sometimes buy a spaghetti squash, cook it, scrape out the insides, which look just like spaghetti, and use it instead of noodles. Until this day I've never told them. I guess if they read this they will now know.

TIP: The pre-cooked bacon now available in stores can get costly but a full package of uncooked may never be used if you are cooking for 1 or 2. Try cooking a full package of bacon until it's almost crispy. Put what you don't use in a freezer bag and store it in the meat keeper of your refrigerator until needed. When ready, place it on a paper towel and microwave until hot, just like the store bought type.

1, 1, 1, 1, 2 Cobbler

1 C. flour
1 C. milk
1 C. sugar
1 stick margarine/butter
2 C. chopped fruit

Whisk together flour, milk, and sugar. Spray an 8x10 casserole dish with non-stick cooking spray. Pour the batter into the dish (it will be very thin). Evenly spread the fruit throughout the batter. Cut the margarine into ¼" pieces and place over the mix. Bake in a 350° oven for about 45 minutes. The batter will rise to the top as it cooks, so to tell if it's done carefully pull some of the crust apart near the center. If you can still see fairly liquid batter, cook a little longer.

> This is the simplest cobbler recipe you will ever find. You can use almost any fruit, with or without juice. The reason I can't be specific as to the time in this recipe or really in any recipe is because different ovens, due to age, heat differently. Some heat hotter, some heat cooler and this will make the cooking time vary. I've also tried this cobbler concept using meat. Of course you would leave out the sugar and might want to add my favorite—cheese. Just use your mind and see what you can create.

TIP: Use non-stick spray in any dish you are cooking in. It really keeps food from sticking and clean-up is a breeze. As you will notice, I use it enough that I probably should buy stock in the companies.

Fried Pickles

1 C. all-purpose flour
½ t. seasoning salt
1 egg
½ C. milk
1 ½ C. thin dill pickle slices, drained
1–2 splashes of hot sauce (optional)
oil for deep frying
ranch dressing for dipping

In a shallow bowl, mix flour and seasonings. In another bowl, whisk the egg, hot sauce, and milk together. Put the pickles on a paper towel and blot them dry. Coat the pickles in the flour, dip into the egg mix, and then in the flour again. Using an electric skillet, deep fryer, or a sauce pan with 2–3 inches of cooking oil heated to 375°, fry about 10 pickles at a time for about 3 minutes or until they are golden brown, turning them once. Drain on a paper towel and serve warm with ranch dressing.

> I really like pickles, almost any kind, but I could not imagine eating them fried. But I'm game for tasting almost anything, and I'm really glad I tried these. I've made them with different cuts of pickles and the thin slices are best. When I made this with spears, you got too much pickle taste. The thin slices create the perfect blend with the batter. These are also good when you sprinkle a little, you got it, parmesan cheese on them while they are still hot. Plus, I've found that pickles are not the only veggies that are good fried. Use this same method and fry up some broccoli.

TIP: Leftover broccoli can be reused by placing it in an ovenproof dish. Pour a can of cream of mushroom or cream of chicken soup over it. Sprinkle with a few cracker crumbs and bake at 350 until bubbly. You can also add cheese.

Mushroom Bread

1 8-oz. tube crescent rolls
½ lb. mushrooms sliced
3 T. olive oil
½ t. Italian seasonings
1 T. minced garlic
½ C. shredded cheese
¼ C. Parmesan cheese

Separate crescent dough, unroll, and place on a pizza pan with points toward center. Toss mushrooms in olive oil to coat. Place evenly over dough. Sprinkle with seasonings, garlic, and cheeses. Bake at 375° for 15–20 minutes, or until crust is golden brown.

> Sometimes I don't want an Italian tasting dish with tomato sauce so I've found a way to solve that little problem. This is a very versatile recipe. You can use sliced cherry tomatoes, onions, bell peppers, actually any veggie you might want on a pizza. This idea came from a bread dish I had while living in Florida. It was called beach bread. Their bread had blue cheese spread over the already cooked bread, diced tomatoes, and cheese. It was then toasted. It was good, but I think mine is better.

TIP: Sauerkraut is something that comes in an oversized container. Try this with leftover sauerkraut. Squeeze out the juice between paper towels. Stuff it, cheese, and any meat you might like into a pita shell and either microwave, toast in toaster oven, or put between a waffle iron. Makes a tasty sandwich.

Pina Colada Salad

1 pineapple, peeled, cored, and chopped into small pieces
1 coconut, drained, shelled, and cut into small pieces
2 kiwi fruit, peeled and chopped into small pieces
1 can frozen pina colada mix

Mix everything together. Refrigerate at least 2–3 hours so the flavors can blend.

My sister and I have a tradition with our daughters. Each year we take them on a trip. We pay for the housing and most of the food. The only thing they have to pay for is their personal shopping. Last year we went to the North Carolina Mountains, and everyone had a great time. This year we are going to the Tennessee Mountains. The trip consists of three generations. Ourselves, our daughters, and my daughter-in-law Amy, and each of the girls bring their children. That gives us about fifteen all together. This year we are doing things a little differently. We pay for the lodging and most of the food, but the meals will be done at the house. Each adult, which includes my sister Net and myself, her two daughters Brandy and Dianna, my two daughters Leslie and Marcia, and my daughter-in-law Amy will be responsible for one meal. We will be there three nights so that works out perfectly. But each meal has to have a theme. Mine is tropical. So what can be more tropical than a pina colada salad. Of course, I'm not sure what I'm going to serve with it, but I have until August and I'm sure something will come up. Try a trip like this with your own family. It not only brings you closer, it also helps you get to know each other.

TIP: Lettuce leaves absorb fat. Place a few into the pot and watch the fat cling to them.

Boiled Peanuts

1 lb. raw peanuts
½ C. salt
enough water to cover peanuts
slow cooker

Pour everything into the slow cooker and turn to high. The peanuts will need to cook for about 8 hours. Replace water as needed.

> I think I told you I'm from Georgia, and boiled peanuts are something we either love or hate. Most of us love them. On one of my trips to visit my daughter Marcia in Jersey, I found out that my significant other had a friend he was in the military with that lived about twenty-five minutes from where my daughter lived. We made arrangements to meet and have dinner. The meal was wonderful and I really enjoyed the company. So, as a thank you, my significant other and I decided to send him a southern care package. He had tasted Cheerwine, which is a cherry cola, but he couldn't buy it in Jersey. So we bought him some Cheerwine. We knew what we wanted to send and that was food straight from the South. We went to a local grocery chain that I knew carried things that would work, in other words things that were really southern, some of which I wouldn't even eat. We found things like black-eyed peas, pickled pigs feet, instant grits, and even brains and eggs. But the one thing we found and he really liked was a can of boiled peanuts. So if you've never tried them, do. You will either love them or hate them.

TIP: If you buy a sweet melon and it isn't really as sweet as you thought it should be, sprinkle a little sugar substitute over it and let it sit for an hour or so. The substitute dissolves quicker than sugar and doesn't take as much.

Salmon Puffs

1 14-oz. can salmon, drained
¼ C. chopped almonds
½ C. water
1 chicken bouillon cube
½ C. oil
½ T. dried parsley
½ C. flour
2 eggs
3–4 dashes hot sauce with garlic

With a fork, mash up salmon. Add almonds and set aside. In a saucepan, combine the water, bouillon, oil, and parsley. Heat to a boil. Add the flour and blend until it makes a ball. Set it off the heat and let it cool to room temperature. After cooling, add the eggs, one at a time, mixing well. Add the hot sauce. Now stir in the salmon and mix well. Drop onto a baking sheet sprayed with non-stick cooking spray. Cook 12–14 minutes at 450°. Makes about 2 dozen.

> I've always loved salmon patties. When I moved my mother close to me in Georgia, I would go by her house every day at lunch to check on her. She would always have something cooked for lunch. And she knew this was my favorite. But as long as she was cooking my salmon patties I never learned how she made them. This was a mistake because when she passed away no one had her recipe. I've searched and experimented for years trying to perfect a salmon patty recipe. They have come out dry inside and out. They have had the taste of bread and not the salmon. I've used everything from cornmeal to flour and still couldn't get them right. These are perfectly crisp on the outside and nice and moist on the inside. You can add onions to this dish but sauté them first

and add them to the salmon mix. This isn't my mother's recipe but the taste is pretty close.

TIP: When using canned salmon you will find some skin still attached to the meat. This won't hurt you, but I always take a spoon and scoop it off.

Breakfast Pinwheels

6 slices bacon, cooked crisp and crumbled
½ C. shredded cheese
2 eggs
1 8-oz. can refrigerated crescent rolls

In a bowl combine bacon, cheese, and eggs. Separate dough into 4 rectangles, sealing perforations on both sides. On each rectangle spread bacon mix to within ¼" of the edges. Roll up jelly-roll style and pinch the end of the dough to seal. Cut into thirds and place on a non-stick sprayed baking dish with the cut side down (like a cinnamon roll). Bake at 375° for 12–15 minutes or until golden brown.

> This is another one of those all-in-one breakfasts. You have egg, bacon, cheese, and bread and can even eat it with your hands. To me this is better than any bacon, egg, and cheese biscuit I've gotten at the fast food stores. The crescent makes it different and tastier by adding just a little sweetness. And of course it can be changed to suite your taste. Use sausage, ham, or any other meat you like. I haven't tried it yet but I think leftover roast would be good. And you don't have to make it just for breakfast. Try eliminating the egg and using tuna salad. Just make sure the filling is chopped small.

TIP: I enjoy crescent rolls in the tube, but when I go to buy them it seems for the money the larger cans are cheaper. So what do you do with the unused ones? They won't keep in the refrigerator; I've tried. They go flat and won't rise. So, roll up 4 of them as they should be. Take the other 4 and mix 2 T. brown sugar and 2 T. crushed drained pineapple and spread it over the leftover crescents and roll up. Bake along with the others. You have bread for dinner as well as something sweet, all in one cooking.

Sausage Noodle Salad

2 C. uncooked noodles
1 lb. bulk sausage, crumbled, fried and drained well
1 C. cheddar cheese
4 boiled eggs
¼ C. mayonnaise
1 T. dill pickle cubes

Cook noodles until soft. In a large bowl put cheese in first, and pour the drained noodles over the cheese while hot to melt the cheese. Add all other ingredients. Stir well. Add more mayonnaise if too dry. Serve hot or cold.

> Sausage is a food I enjoy. Many times I'll make a sausage burger instead of a beef burger. I make it the same way I do any burger. Put it on a bun, add mustard, catsup, mayo, pickles, and lettuce. It's so good that sometimes I would rather have it than beef burgers. So while I was making up this recipe I did some thinking. I like tuna salad and chicken salad made this way, so why not sausage. I took this to one of my testers to try and she really liked it. I then took it to another one to try and her son and daughter-in-law were there and fussed because I didn't bring enough for them. So what do I do? I go home, put the rest of my new dish in a bowl and take it to them to take home. I think my tester numbers are growing.

TIP: When making soups that call for noodles, they sometimes come out soggy. Cook them separately and add when the soup is done. Don't forget to salt the noodles.

Creamy Slaw

2 C. cabbage, grated
2 t. vinegar
2 t. sugar
onion
mayonnaise
salt and pepper to taste

After grating the cabbage into a bowl, run an onion over the grater three or four times. This will give you more juice than actual onion but the juice is strong. Add the vinegar and sugar and mix together. Add enough mayo to make the slaw creamy. Start with 1 T. and mix, add more if needed. Salt and pepper to taste.

The first condo cookout I attended was on the Fourth of July and hosted by a friend who lived there. Everyone was to bring a dish or two, and I chose the potato salad and slaw. After tasting my slaw it was made official that after I moved in I would be the one to bring the potato salad and slaw to all cookouts and gatherings. If you find you want more onion flavor, run the onion over the grater a couple of times more, but again remember the juice is stronger than chopped onions. And as for the sugar and vinegar, the sugar tones down the vinegar and the vinegar tones down the sugar so use it in equal parts. You can also add grated carrots, and I've even substituted the cabbage for broccoli stalks. It won't be as creamy but it has more crunch. Just take the stalks of fresh broccoli and cut off the outer edge or you will have a salad that eats like grated wood. You will be able to tell when you get to the tender part of the stalk. Grate it like you do cabbage and then follow the rest of the recipe. And if you are not a broccoli fan, it doesn't really taste like broccoli when you're finished. Try it; you might like something new.

TIP: Use a potato peeler to slice cheese paper thin.

Chicken with Saffron Rice

3 chicken breasts, cooked and cubed
2 pkg. saffron flavored rice, cooked according to package directions
½ C. sour cream
1 can cream of chicken soup
½ can of milk
Ritz crackers

Spray the bottom and sides of a 2 qt. casserole dish. Crush about ¾ a sleeve of the crackers and sprinkle them on the bottom of the dish. Mix the chicken, rice, sour cream, soup, and milk together and place on top of the crackers. Crush about ½ a sleeve of the crackers and sprinkle them on top of the chicken. Spray the crackers with non-stick cooking spray and bake in a 350° oven for about 20 minutes, or until crackers are golden brown.

> My daughter Leslie has been bragging about her chicken casserole for a long time. I had some chicken breasts thawed out for dinner one night and e-mailed her to get her recipe. She was right about it being good. I've racked my brain trying to come up with a way to change it or add to it but it's too perfect to change. Well, maybe a few almond slivers mixed into the chicken mix. Or possibly some cheese. Or maybe some chopped broccoli. You could add these but it's really perfect as it is. It makes a lot but my testers seemed to be happy that it did when I took samples over to them. And I even saved enough to take for my lunch the next day.

TIP: To clean a microwave oven, boil a cup of water inside the microwave and let it sit for a few minutes with the door closed. You'll be able to wipe it clean with no scrubbing.

Coconut Custard Bars

1 C. sugar
¼ C. margarine/butter
4 eggs
½ C. self-rising flour
2 C. milk
1 t. vanilla
1 C. coconut

Using a mixer, blend all ingredients together at one time. Pour into a large pie plate sprayed with non-stick cooking spray. Bake for 1 hour at 350°.

This recipe isn't really a pie but you can cook it in a pie pan. You can also cook it in muffin pans and they only take about 20–30 minutes to bake. I've even made it in a square casserole dish and baked it the full hour. It makes its own crust so you don't have to make or buy one. It has enough eggs in it to qualify as custard, but it's firm enough to cut into bars. If you're ever looking for something quick and easy to prepare, you can't beat this. Now to change it a little. How about some nuts or maybe some chocolate chips or in my case white chocolate chips? Or possibly some well-drained pineapple?

TIP: To keep icing from running off a cake, dust it with cornstarch.

No Flour Peanut Butter Chocolate Cookies

1 C. creamy peanut butter
1 ½ C. sugar
1 egg
1 t. vanilla
2 dozen milk chocolate candies

Preheat oven to 350°. Mix peanut butter, sugar, egg, and vanilla together in a bowl. Roll into 1 ½" balls. With a fork, press out to flatten. Put one piece of candy in the center of each. Bake 12 minutes. Makes 2 dozen.

> I'm a sucker for a sale at the grocery store. And the six baskets that stared at me shortly after walking into my favorite store was proof of my weakness. It was shortly after Easter and they had everything from stuffed animals to candy on sale for 75% off. That's a great buy! So I picked up several packages of name brand chocolate. You know, those little ones that are individually wrapped in foil. I think I bought five bags, and I don't even like chocolate. But since they were so cheap I knew I could find a use for them. A few nights later I was watching my favorite food show and one of the cooks was making no flour peanut butter cookies. So I can't take credit for this recipe, but I can take credit for finding something to do with those 75% off candies. I put them on the cookies. I've found this works well with any candy that goes with peanut butter. I've tried the candies with nuts in them and some with caramel inside, they were on sale too so I had to try; they all work great.

TIP: When the holiday seasons are over, seasonal candies go on sale. This is a good time to buy. They will keep for several months un-opened.

Potato Broccoli with Salsa Cheese

1 8-oz. jar cheese dip with salsa
¼ C. milk
4 medium potatoes, cubed
1 10-oz. pkg. frozen broccoli
salt and pepper to taste

Spray a 13x9 baking dish. Mix the cheese dip and milk until blended. Pour into the dish. Top with potatoes and broccoli. Salt and pepper to taste. Cover dish with foil. Bake in 350° oven for 30–40 minutes or until potatoes are soft. Serves 4–6.

> My potato broccoli dish started out as a pork chop casserole. I did everything just as I've instructed but I also browned some pork chops and put them on top of the broccoli. It looked great, and I couldn't wait to taste it. Well, sometimes we do well, sometimes we fail, and sometimes we just don't make a difference. The pork chops ended up tasting like plain old pork chops that had been browned. No special taste at all. I really thought the salsa in the cheese would at least give them some flavor. Nope. So then I tried the potatoes and broccoli. They were great. The salsa made a difference in them. I put a little pat of butter on top of my serving and didn't bother with the chops.

TIP: When making scrambled eggs, use sour cream instead of milk. It keeps the eggs moist and creamy.

Hash Brown Potatoes Au Gratin

½ C. milk
½ C. canned cream
4 medium potatoes, grated (rinse, drain, and squeeze dry in paper towel)
2 T. margarine
1 C. grated cheddar cheese

Heat the milk and cream in a sauce pan on medium heat. Don't use high; it will cause the milk to stick. Add potatoes and margarine, and simmer slowly until thickened and potatoes are tender. Pour into sprayed baking dish. Sprinkle with cheese. Place under boiler and broil until cheese is lightly brown. Serves 6–8.

> I really like hash browns. Anytime I go out for breakfast and they offer hash browns, I order them over anything else. I've tried for years to make them at home but they were always soft and mushy and never browned until I discovered the secret: rinse, drain, and squeeze dry. Now I can have them anytime I want. And of course cheese being an important staple in my cooking, I had to find a way to add it to my hash browns. This dish, too, can be improved on. Add sautéed onions, bell peppers, and/or salsa to the hash browns before pouring them into the baking dish. You could even add some crispy cooked bacon. The additions are only as short as your imagination.

TIP: When a recipe calls for graham cracker crumbs and butter combined, pour the crumbs into a heavy duty plastic bag, then pour in the melted butter. Close the bag and use your fingers to blend the crumbs and butter. Pour into your dish and throw away the bag.

Shrimp and Rice Pilaf

8 pieces bacon, fried crisp
2 C. cooked rice
½ lb. shrimp, peeled and cut into small pieces
1 can cream of mushroom soup

Using the same pan you fried the bacon in, pour off all but about 1 T. of grease and add the shrimp. Sauté on medium heat until pink. Add the soup and continue to cook on medium heat until hot. Fold in the rice and place in a serving bowl. Crumble the bacon and sprinkle on top. Serves 4.

> The day I made this recipe I had been experimenting with oven-cooked onion rings. I had just thrown out two large onions and four different kinds of possible batters. The first one I tried was done with crumbled corn flakes. One taste and I found it tasted too much like corn flakes with a little onion. In the trash. The second one I tried with rice flour. I used an egg wash and then dipped the rings into the rice flour. In the trash. I tried wetting the rice flour. Have you ever seen the baby food that comes in a box that you add milk to? Now I know why babies make such a face when trying to eat it. In the trash. Next came failure number four. I tried using my shrimp batter, which is made of flour and cornstarch. In the trash. Onions are cheap compared to shrimp and after four failures with my baked onion rings I was a little worried about working on something that had shrimp in it. I guess for me the fifth try was a winner. The shrimp and rice pilaf is really good. Now I'm thinking of ways to change and/or improve. Almonds, cheese, sweet peas, broccoli. Need I go on?

TIP: To keep oils from leaving a mess on the shelves, use paper-lined aluminum cupcake holders as coasters under the bottles.

Fried Squash Patties

1 C. grated yellow squash
2 t. grated onions
2 T. melted butter
3 T. flour
1 egg, beaten
salt and pepper to taste
oil for cooking

Mix all ingredients, adding the egg last. Drop by spoonfuls into a skillet hot with oil and brown on both sides.

> When I was a kid I hated squash. And I had the misfortune of growing up in a family where you sat at the table until your plate was empty. When the dog was in the house it wasn't usually a problem. But when my parents found out why the dog was getting so fat they would make sure he stayed in another room during meals. I sat at the table one Sunday from lunch until dinner because I wouldn't eat my squash. I finally learned to do what other kids with the same problem did and that was to hold my nose, put the spoon of squash as far back in my throat as possible, and swallow. I didn't seem to taste it as much. I think that's because your taste glands are in the front of your mouth. Now I still am not crazy about squash, but if I can make it in a way that it doesn't look like squash and doesn't really taste like squash, I'll eat it. This I like.

TIP: Use flat bottom ice cream cones to serve pudding. It will sit flat on the table or they can take it outside and won't need a spoon. This works with tuna and chicken salad too.

Bacon, Egg, and Cheese Mini Pies

6–8 pieces of bacon, cooked crisp and crumbled
3 eggs
½ C. cheddar cheese
½ C. mozzarella cheese
1 tube flaky biscuits

Spray a mini-muffin pan with non-stick spray. Pull the biscuits apart making three out of each. Press each into a muffin tin, bringing it up around the sides. Mix all other ingredients and spoon about 1 T. into each biscuit. Bake at 375° for 12–15 minutes, or until egg is set.

> Even when my kids were young I enjoyed working with new recipes and creating my own. I would go through magazines, never reading the articles. I never really bought them for the articles, but for the recipes. I would find one I liked and thought my family would like, cut it out, put it in a box I kept sorted by type—meats, veggies, etc., and at random once a week, I would pull out a recipe, go to the store, buy everything it took to make it, including the pan if I didn't have it, and cook it up. When I served it to my family I would ask each to rate it from one to ten. If it got an eight or better I would transfer it to a card, mark its rating on the card, store it in another box, and end up making it again. This not only gave me new foods to cook but it also stocked my cabinet with the tools to make them. This is the same method I've used with my testers. They rate the food and that determines if it's cookbook worthy. The recipe above received a fifteen out of ten. It turned out that good. And of course, you can use sausage, ham, or no meat at all. You could even put a little drained salsa in it if you like.

TIP: If you have a problem keeping boiled eggs separate from uncooked eggs, put a drop or two of food coloring in the water.

This will tint the eggs and there will be no mistake as to which are uncooked and which are boiled.

Pina Colada Cake

1 pudding cake mix
3 whole eggs
1 can coconut milk
½ C. water

Mix all of the above and bake in a 9x13 sheet cake pan sprayed with non-stick cooking spray until a toothpick inserted into the center comes out clean. Punch holes in the top of the cake with a straw while still hot.

Icing:

1 can sweetened condensed milk
1 C. coconut milk
1 small can crushed pineapple, drained
coconut

Mix all condensed milk, coconut milk, and pineapple until smooth. Drizzle over warm cake, letting it seep into the holes made with the straw. Sprinkle with coconut.

> Cutting up whole pineapple isn't hard. There are usually directions attached to show you how. Coconut is another story. First you punch holes in the "eyes." These are easy to find. I use a clean nail and hammer to drain the "milk." When I was a kid I loved drinking the coconut milk. Still do. After draining, wrap the coconut in an old towel, take it outside where there is a hard surface, hopefully concrete, hit it hard with the hammer. Keep hitting until you have pieces no bigger than maybe 4." Next take a blunt knife and press it under the edge of the coconut and shell to loosen the pieces.

They will usually pop off the shell fairly easily. Now you will see a brown "crust" still attached to the coconut. This has to come off. I do this with a knife but please be careful and don't cut yourself. If you follow these directions carefully you can enjoy fresh coconut.

TIP: Dip spoon in hot water before measuring butter. It will slip off the spoon more easily.

Crusty Baked Chicken Breasts

1 C. breadcrumbs
½ C. grated Parmesan cheese
3 t. minced garlic
2 T. olive oil
4 boneless, skinless chicken breasts
¼ C. minced fresh basil
¼ C. mayonnaise

Preheat oven to 425°. Combine breadcrumbs, Parmesan, garlic, and oil. Pat chicken dry with paper towels and transfer to 9x13 baking dish. Combine basil and mayonnaise in small bowl and spread mixture evenly over chicken. Sprinkle breadcrumb mixture over mayonnaise, pressing lightly to adhere. Bake 18–22 minutes.

> My sister and her soon-to-be husband will be living in my condo complex. They were painting and getting everything ready to move in one night, and since I didn't help her paint I thought the least I could do was cook dinner for them. That's when I made this Crusty Chicken. I went simple with the meal making rice, gravy which was actually made from a can of cream of mushroom soup with a little sage added, steamed broccoli, and biscuits. My brother-in-law Rick loved it and kept telling my sister Net that she had to get the recipe. He ate a full serving of everything and took the leftovers home to not eat the next day but later that night. This can be changed by cooking the chicken on a bed of rice, adding the broccoli to the chicken, or eat it the way Rick did, add gravy to all of it.

TIP: Fresh breadcrumbs are easy to make. 2 slices of bread put into a food processor makes 1 cup of breadcrumbs. Seasons can be added when processing.

Index

Breads

Desserts

Fruit

Meats

Miscellaneous

Veggies